MEMORIES *of a* RELUCTANT SOLDIER

THE COLD WAR REVISITED

Bruce Conroe

ISBN: 978-1-4834-2695-2 (sc)
ISBN: 978-1-4834-2696-9 (e)

Lulu Publishing Services rev. date: 03/13/2015

DEDICATION

This work is dedicated to the memory of Barbara Holme Conroe (1931-2013), my friend for 77 years, my sweetheart for much of that time, and my beloved wife for 59 years. She was the best thing that ever happened to me. Our once-in-a-lifetime love carried us through years of highs and lows - both of us enjoying the ride.

The chapters dealing with our time in the US Army will demonstrate her selflessness. She could have stayed home with her parents the whole two years, but she refused to do that. Without knowing the living conditions in West Germany and the discomfort that would be involved, she insisted in going overseas to be with me and have our first child there. She would not allow me to spend the first year of our son's life away from him. I will always be exceedingly grateful to her.

This was written for our children Scott, David, Laurie and John

and for their children, Aura, Jenna, Kaylie,
Ryan, Emilee and Allison.

With love,
Dad/Papa

Introduction

We hear a lot about the veterans of World War II, the Korean Conflict, and the Vietnam War, but little mention is made, these days, of the Cold War. It was 40 years of tensions, spying, a nuclear race and competition in space between 1949 and 1989, the era of the Berlin Wall. It included the Korean Conflict of 1950-1953 and the Vietnam War of 1964-1972. This monograph was written to remind people of that era and the many times other than Korea and Vietnam that the United States and Russia stared each other down on the brink of battles that, luckily, did not occur.

This is also the story of one drafted soldier, whose regiment was guarding the Czech border of West Germany against any possible military movement along the 172 miles of that front. This was especially tense in October of 1956 when the Hungarians revolted against communist control, and the Suez crisis occurred in Egypt and the Sinai peninsula.

It is also written for the benefit of younger generations, especially our children, and their understanding of the seemingly world wide conflict between communism and democracy.

I am grateful to several friends and family members who read drafts of the manuscript and made positive suggestions for the flow and readability of the story. This was especially important in the description of the two years of my US Army "career." Thank you one and all.

Bruce Conroe, October,2014

PROLOGUE

Regensburg, Bavaria, West Germany

October 1956

The four companies of the 3rd Battalion, 6th Armored Cavalry Regiment, are moving sedately down a country road, headed for a specific rendezvous with other elements of the Regiment and the US 7th Army. From the serious demeanor of the soldiers and the close lineup of their vehicles, it is hard to tell if this is just another alert, a practice exercise, or a real foray into combat. This close to the Czechoslovakian border, it could be that the Czechs have finally moved into West Germany. The Hungarian Uprising occurred this month, and the Czechs might think it is a good time for them to act, also. Unlike an infantry unit, all personnel in an armored cavalry are assigned to a vehicle. Our column consisting of tanks, jeeps, trucks and personnel carriers passes through small Bavarian villages with their red tiled roofs and onion domed churches, ordinarily colorful and bustling with activity. The tanks make a rumbling and squeaky noise as the long line moves ahead, with the air heavy with the smells of engine emission. But it is early morning. The house wives (haus fraus) are beginning their daily housekeeping chores, and the village green is quiet as we enter and turn a right angle into the center of the village. As the I Company Supply Clerk, I am riding in the 2 and ½ ton supply truck (commonly called a "deuce and a half" in Army parlance). The truck is driven by our regular driver, a corporal, and our Supply Sergeant sits beside him. I am perched high above them in the machine gun ring (literally a circular track about 4 feet in diameter that the gun slides on), manning the 50 caliber gun. From here, I can see clearly that the townspeople are upset by our passage.

They don't know if this is real war or a practice alert. One woman captures my attention as she leans out of a second story window, heaving the feather bed across the sill to air. I can see the fear on her face as she freezes in that pose, aware that this could be our response to a real attack from the Barischerwald (Bavarian woods) Mountains to the east and a return to the war that ended for Germany twelve years ago.

It is, in fact, another practice alert. At this point in the Cold War, the world is in turmoil. American troops are still a huge presence in South Korea after the "conflict" ended in 1953. The Suez crisis kept the world on edge this month and has now been resolved. Although the occupation of Germany has ended, American troops maintain the responsibility for the security of West Germany as a constabulary and are vigilant while watching the situation in Hungary.

Earlier this year, Europe was struggling with an extraordinarily harsh winter and higher tension of the Cold War. West Germany regained its sovereignty in May of 1955, but still has only the bare beginning of its own army while American troops continue to police and defend it. Having been drafted into the Army, I have only a few months left of my two years and look forward to my departure with my wife and son, hoping that the Iron Curtain will not erupt. We are constantly tense, in the midst of the otherwise picturesque scenery, "we" being US Army personnel, particularly those of the 6th Armored Cavalry. Our task is to patrol West Germany's eastern border, which is a normally calm piece of Europe, with rolling hills and quiet woods, that could erupt into an active war zone.

CHAPTER ONE

World War II Ends

Most people, by now, have forgotten or choose to ignore that the Cold War existed. It was the longest war in United States history (46 years) and extended worldwide. It was a battle of wills and high tension overall, but did include the Korean Conflict and the Vietnam War. These both were the result of the suspicions, spying and one-up-man-ship that occurred around the globe. One only has to study a real globe and then follow the events of 1945-1991 to see the international scope of the Cold War, even though the major highlighted tensions were those between the USSR and the USA.

It all began with the defeat of Germany in 1945 that ended the war in Europe. In February of that year, the leaders of Great Britain, France, the USSR and the USA met at Yalta on the Black Sea to discuss the occupation of the defeated European countries. They agreed on making 4 divisions of Germany, each under the control of one of the above nations. They also agreed that all nations held by Nazi Germany should have free elections. At this same time the United Nations organization replaced the failed League of Nations. In press coverage of this event, reporters mentioned the frailty of US President Franklin D. Roosevelt. In addition to years of poliomyelitis he seemed to be suffering also from physical weakness and fatigue.

On April 12th (my 14th birthday), President Roosevelt suffered a massive stroke while on vacation in Warm Springs, GA, where he maintained a home. He often went there to rest and take advantage of the healing springs. This death was a huge blow to the American people and, indeed, to the Allied nations. We who were young teenagers had never known another President, so we reacted questioningly, "What will happen now?" Of course the adults knew the answer. Vice President Harry S. Truman would take over. Many thought he hadn't the experience to take control, but he was sworn that same day.

Unfortunately, Roosevelt and his inner circle had kept Truman out of the loop, so he had little knowledge of the inner workings of the Cabinet to help him. We were to see him take hold confidently and lead us to the close of the rest of the War.

August was a pivotal month that year. Germany had surrendered in May, so that the four leading Allies held another conference at Potsdam, Germany, which ended August 2. There was a different cast of players this time with President Truman replacing FDR They firmed up the division of Germany and subdivided Berlin as well. They also agreed to start legal trials of Nazi war criminals in Nuremberg. On August 6th, President Truman gave permission for the first use of the atomic bomb. Hiroshima, Japan, was the target for the purpose of ending the war quickly to avoid thousands more American casualties. A second bomb was dropped on Nagasaki, Japan, which immediately brought the end of the Second World War. Japan surrendered on August 14, followed by formal signatures in September aboard the USS Missouri in the presence of General Douglas MacArthur.

Another key event in the emerging Cold War was the defection on September 5 of a clerk in the Russian embassy in Ottawa, Canada.

He provided proof to the Royal Canadian Mounted Police of a Soviet spy ring active in Canada and other western countries. This changed the perception of the USSR from being an ally to now becoming a foe. Friendly Uncle Joe Stalin wasn't friendly after all, and thus began the many years of Communism versus Democracy.

The remaining years of the 1940's decade were not as dramatic, but led to more mistrust, spying and smaller conflicts. But some major events at the end of the decade were very worrying. The following examples show that troubles were brewing in various parts of the globe.

In January 1946, the Chinese Civil War resumed with battles between Communist and Nationalist armies.

On January 7th the Republic of Austria was reconstituted, but, like Germany, divided into four sectors controlled by the same powers.

In March the Greek Civil War reignited between communists and the conservative Greek government.

On March 5, in a speech at Westminster College in Missouri (he was invited there to the President's home state by Mr. Truman), Winston Churchill warned the audience of the descent of an "Iron Curtain" across Europe.

During this time, several countries discontinued their monarchies and several countries discontinued colonial ownerships.

December 19 marked the beginning of the First Indochina War with the landings of French forces in Indochina.

The year 1947 began with the American and British zones of Germany being united, forming what was called a Bizone.

On April 16, Barnard Baruch gave a speech at the unveiling of his portrait in the South Carolina House of Representatives in which he used the term "Cold War" for the first time while describing how matters stood between the US and the USSR.

In Europe, on July 11, the US announced new occupation policies for Germany. These were based on the premise that, for Europe to prosper, Germany's economy needed to prosper.

Switching our attention to Asia, on August 14, India and Pakistan were granted independence by the United Kingdom. Then, a month later, the UN passed a resolution calling for withdrawal of foreign soldiers from Korea and also formed a commission to concentrate on the unification of that peninsula.

The next year brought very serious events, and escalating tensions in several locations, including the US. First, in February, the Communist Party seized control of Czechoslovakia.

On April 3, 1948, President Truman signed the Marshall Plan with programs aiding many European countries. By the time that program ended, the US had given $12.4 billion in economic assistance.

On June 24 Joseph Stalin of the USSR ordered the blockade of all land routes from West Germany to Berlin. The intent of this dramatic move was to starve out the French, British and American forces from the city. Those three nations then launched the Berlin Airlift to supply the citizens of Berlin. They defeated the blockade by May 11, 1949.

In July, the constitution of the Republic of Korea became effective. Then two months later, the Soviet Union announced that the Democratic People's Republic of Korea was the legitimate government of the total Korea.

On November 20, the American consul and his staff in Mukden, China, were forced into virtual captivity by Chinese communist forces. This did not end for a year, which meant that relations between the US and the communist government of China were seriously strained, to say the least.

Now we arrive at 1949, the final year of the 1940's decade. Everyone continued to hope for a better year on this planet, but the tensions (that's probably an understatement) kept building. It should be mentioned that the military drafting of young men still continued. On April 4 the North Atlantic Treaty Organization (NATO) was created by twelve nations, including the United States, for the purpose of fending off communist expansion on the globe.

April 12 was my 18th birthday. Yes, I immediately registered with Selective Service System (the draft) by visiting my guidance counselor's office at school.

Good news! On May 11 the Soviet blockade of Berlin ended with the re-opening of access routes. However, the airlift was continued until September in case there was a change of mind in the Kremlin.

May 23 marked the merger of the Bizone and the French zone in Germany to form the Federal Republic of Germany (commonly referred to as West Germany) with Bonn designated as the capital. Conrad Adenauer was the first Chancellor.

In the United States, a congressional committee had been searching out Communist sympathizers among the citizenry (referred to as the Red Scare). It came to a peak in June with fingers pointed at American celebrities, including Hollywood stars.

On October 1, the People's Republic of China was announced. This added a quarter of the world's population to the communist bloc.

Then on October 7 the Soviet Union declared their zone of Germany to be the German Democratic Republic, with its capital being East Berlin.

October 7 also marked the end of the Greek Civil War, declared by the Communist Party leader there. This was considered a successful "containment" of the spread of communism.

In December, the Netherlands returned sovereignty to the United States of Indonesia following the Dutch-Indonesian Round Table Conference.

CHAPTER TWO

The Tensions Explode

The decade of the 1950s encompassed enough Cold War events to be a separate book or speech. This was a very tumultuous and worrying time. The tension escalated immediately with the January 5, 1950, recognition of the Peoples' Republic of China by the United Kingdom. This caused the Republic of China under General Chiang Kai-Shek to sever diplomatic relations with the UK and move its capital to Taipei, Taiwan.

On June 25th of the same year, North Korea invaded South Korea opening the Korean War. Three days later, Seoul, the capital of South Korea, fell to the North Koreans. Then on the 30th, the United Nations agreed to send forces to aid South Korea.

In July, United Nations forces engaged the North Koreans for the first time, halting the North Korean advance. The United States then stepped up the Selective Service process to draft more men for participation in the UN forces. Across the country young men in college completed an academic abilities examination so that their draft boards could decide on college deferments. This was at the end of my Freshman year at Alfred University, in Alfred, NY. While I never saw my score on the exam, I was deferred to continue my studies.

At the end of September, United Nations forces defeated North Korean armed forces, then pressed on and recaptured Seoul. October of 1950 was a time of major activity in the War. UN troops crossed the 38th parallel into North Korea, and forces of the Peoples' Republic of China appeared formidably along the Yalu River. Then the North Korean capital of Pyongyang was captured by United Nations armies. Next, 300,000 soldiers of Red China intervened in a surprise move, but they withdrew after only one engagement.

In mid-November, UN forces approached the Yalu River causing China to intervene again, but with 500,000 soldiers that time. This forced UN armies back toward South Korea. At the very beginning of 1951, the Chinese captured Seoul followed in mid-March by UN forces recapturing it and advancing to the 38th parallel, thereby creating a defensive barrier across the whole peninsula.

As Spring arrived, our attention was drawn to various locations on the planet. On March 29th, Julius and Ethel Rosenberg were convicted in the US of espionage for passing atomic secrets to the Soviets both during and after World War II. In April, President Truman fired General Douglas MacArthur from commanding the US forces in Korea, and the European Coal and Steel Community was formed by the Treaty of Paris.

April 28, 1952, marked the formal end of our occupation and isolation of Japan by the signing of the Treaty of San Francisco and the Treaty of Taipei. On June 30, the Marshal Plan ended as the European industrial production was found to exceed that of 1938. In July, Gamal Abdel Nasser led a coup against Egypt's King Farouk. October brought the successful testing of the United Kingdom's atomic bomb, while on November 1st the USA tested its first thermonuclear bomb.

The next year, 1953, was another cliff-hanger. It was a time of another change in the makeup of the group determining diplomatic directions. Dwight Eisenhower became the US President in January, and Joseph Stalin died in March, leaving no replacement for five months. The most important event of the year for the world was the end of the Korean War in June, the same month that I graduated from Alfred University with a BA in mathematics. The armistice agreement was signed in July. I received another deferment from the draft in order to proceed to study for a Master's degree at Alfred.

On August 19, the US Central Intelligence Agency (CIA) assisted a royalist coup in Iran that ousted Prime Minister Mosadegh and brought the Shah back into leadership. This was triggered by Iranian nationalization of its oil industry and the fear that Iran would join the Communist movement. It seems we were at odds with Iran even in the 1950's.

August 22 marked my marriage to my high school sweetheart in Albany, New York. We were close friends since Kindergarten and seriously in love by senior year of college, after dating others at our separate colleges. More about our life together will come in a later chapter.

On the heels of our honeymoon and relocation to Alfred, NY, in September Nikita Khrushchev became the leader of the Soviet Communist Party, replacing Joseph Stalin By the way, his chief rival for the position, Laventry Beria, was executed in December.

While the events of 1953 caused increased tension, 1954 brought even more worries, keeping us on edge and unable to decide which ones were more influential on world peace because of their seeming lack of relation to each other. In January, the United States launched its first nuclear submarine, the USS Nautilus, giving us a significant deterrent for any nuclear threats.

In May, the Viet Minh defeated the French at Dien Bien Phu causing the French to leave Indochina. This meant that there were then four independent states there - Cambodia, Laos, and North and South Vietnam. The Geneva Accords called for elections to unite the two Vietnams. However, this did not happen because the major world powers worried that the Viet Minh (Nationalist Communists) would win.

In June, 1954, the Red Scare (concern that some high profile people in the US were members of the Communist Party) escalated with the declaration by US Senator Joseph McCarthy that there were communists in the CIA and in our atomic weapons development. He was Chair of the Un-American Activities Committee and, by now, a household name through live television coverage of the Committee's hearings. On June 18, the leftist Guatemalan government was removed by a CIA supported coup. A rightist regime was installed, followed by guerilla warfare, but the government survived it and stayed in power throughout the Cold War. On June 23, Gamel Abdel Nasser ousted Egypt's King Farouk and established a neutralist government.

In August, the Taiwan Strait crisis began when Chinese Communists shelled the islands of Taiwan (the Republic of China). The US backed Taiwan and the whole thing ended when neither side wanted to press it. (On a personal note, my wife, Barbara and I moved to North Syracuse, NY where I taught math to five classes of 7th and 8th graders.) Getting back to the world scene, September also brought the foundation of the South East Asian Treaty Organization (SEATO). Like NATO, it was expected to resist Communist expansion in the Philippines. Its members were Australia, France, Pakistan, New Zealand, Thailand, the Philippines, the United Kingdom, and the United States.

In December, I received notice that I was being drafted into the US Army the next month.

CHAPTER THREE

Uncle Sam Wants Me

Albany, New York

December 1954

Looking back, I am always reminded of the Charles Dickens book (A Tale of Two Cities) that I had read in college English Lit that it was the best of times full of life and potential, and the worst of times full of worry. It really was the best, being in one's twenties, just out of college, happily married and starting a career with many years ahead. The Korean Conflict had ended, but the Cold War was fully engaged in Europe and elsewhere, and the Selective Service System was watching over young men in this country. They finally caught up with me at Christmas time in 1954 with orders to report for duty on January 7th, 1955. That sure knocked the fun out of the holidays.

I had thought that I could stay unnoticed by the Draft Board, especially if I didn't wave my name at them in the form of an address change, but that was naïve. Barbara and I had graduated from college in 1953 and were married that summer. During the academic year 1953-54, we lived in Alfred, New York - me completing a Master's degree in education at Alfred University and she working as a clerk in the University Registrar's Office.

By the fall of 1954 I had taken a position as a 7th and 8th grade mathematics teacher in North Syracuse, New York, and we blithely proceeded with that plan without telling the Draft Board. I found out later that I would have been exempt if they had known I was teaching mathematics. So the Draft notice awaited us when we went to visit our parents in the outlying area of Albany, NY, for Christmas. Starting with the ominous words that a group of my friends and neighbors had chosen me, I was to report to the Army's recruiting office in Albany on January 7, 1955.

Basically, what this meant was that the US Army would be in control of our lives for the next two years. From January 1955 through December 1956 that was the case. The school district would be required by law to give me back a teaching post at the end of that time.

For both sets of parents, this was not a total shock, so we all planned how we would store our belongings and what Barbara would do. The latter of those was easiest in that her parents invited her to live with them until I completed basic training and learned where I would be stationed. We would store some of our things with my parents in Altamont, NY, our bedroom set with my brother and his wife in Corning, NY, and the remainder with Barbara's parents, Furman and Irene Holme, in Delmar, NY.

So, back we went to North Syracuse to pack and give notice to the High School, where I was assured that, according to law, there would be a job for me when this was over in two years. I taught most of a week as we packed, moved the bedroom set to Corning and then loaded a rental truck, taking furniture to the Conroes in Altamont, and then on to the Holmes, with a few pieces of furniture, several boxes and a brand new automatic clothes washer. All worked according to plan, and we prepared for my departure.

We were a little jittery when we awoke Friday, January 7th, and made an early drive into Albany for Barbara to drop me off at the Draft Board. With an emotional and nervous farewell, I carried a small bag of a few basic clothes plus toiletries up the steps and into a din of about 50 young men's voices. Many of them were from the Albany area, but there was also a large group from Worcester, Massachusetts. Conversations centered around how "lucky" it was we had been drafted before January 31st. On that date, the Korean GI Bill would expire, leaving all of us without those educational and other benefits.

Next came registration and physicals. When a doctor said I had excess curvature of the spine, I asked if that meant I was 4F. "No, keep going", he said. After poking us and examining us in detail, we got dressed and were taken to the Albany train station (now owned by the City of Albany) for travel to New York City on the way to Fort Dix, New Jersey.

CHAPTER FOUR

Basic Training

Fort Dix, NJ January-March 1955

After the bus pulled in to Fort Dix, we were herded into a wooden World War II barracks for bunk assignments in double deck cots and then fed in a nearby mess hall, which bore the sign "Take what you want but eat all you take". I took a top bunk, having no fear of falling out. This was also to my advantage later. We all went to bed in the unheated barracks after discovering that the bathroom had no hot water. Over the next few days we were issued uniforms, which was a godsend for the shivering group. One bit of humor could be found in the fact that when they measured my waist of 30 inches they deliberately gave me pants of waist 28 inches. Still, It was a relief to have two winter uniforms of brown worsted, two summer uniforms of tan khaki, two sets of olive green fatigues, two pairs of brown boots, a pair of brown shoes, olive green overcoat, olive green field jacket, an olive green wool shirt for winter combat, two pairs of gloves (one leather, one knit), two different shades of brown neckties, differing hats for each uniform, and assorted socks and underwear, including long Johns. The hats were two flat tops in olive green to match fatigues, two khaki caps for summer known as "fore-and-aft" caps in the Navy, and a brown dress hat for the winter worsteds and a beige dress hat for summer. All of that, and we were issued large olive green duffel bags (with our names and serial numbers stenciled down the side) to keep it all in when moving to a new location.

Next, we were given various medical shots. The tetanus shot really caused pain in the shoulder, but I found that I could lay my new (and very warm) overcoat up on my upper bunk and back into it. Time spent thinking ahead really paid off in that environment.

There were several new things to learn and learn fast. How, when and whom to salute, how to answer roll call - when your last name was called answer with first name, middle initial and service number. CONROE - -Bruce A. US51318564. How to "blouse" your pant legs in the tops of combat boots (elastic cords helped but some used condoms) How to time yourself getting indoors to avoid standing rigidly at salute while the flag was being lowered for the night. AND never to go outdoors without a "cover" (hat). Oh yes, we also learned how to change clothes quickly from fatigues to dress uniform or the other way in ten minutes. Still a valuable skill!!.

After the traditional drastically short haircut, we were assigned to an Infantry company housed in a new cement and glass barracks with hot water and its own mess hall along with a large lounge (day room) on the first floor. The second and third floors housed rows of double deck bunks in 2 vast areas on each floor. We began training - up at 4:30, shaving and dressing, breakfast, and then marching to classes where we sat outdoors for instruction. I should mention the daily inspection of our bunk areas, which was not hard to prepare, but I learned the hard way to not be too efficient in getting ready fast. The reason? Then you would be assigned to swab down the bathroom. Along the way, I also learned to eat fast and get out of the mess hall. The last ones there had to clean the place.

14

Now assigned to a company, we were issued field gear to learn how to live in battle conditions. We were given a full pack of sleeping bag, tent half that you connected to somebody else's to make a pup tent, an entrenching tool for digging a foxhole, a mess kit, and a wide belt from which hung a canteen and a pouch for rifle ammunition. During this period of sweaty marching to classes (sitting outside in the cold, damp air) We learned how to dismantle and clean the 30 caliber machine gun and the M1 rifle, calisthenics, map orientation, Army protocol, how to make military moves in close order drill including with a rifle on the right shoulder, and parade marching, also with a rifle. My Boy Scout training in close order marching and compass orientation helped me a lot. We also learned bayonet defense and how to crawl close to the ground under machine gun fire.

Calisthenics included running as well as various exercises to build our strength and endurance. That was good for me. I was 5 feet 9 inches tall and weighed 148 pounds. I had good strong legs, but very little upper body muscle. The Army cured all of that. Later in the 8 weeks we would get into firing our rifles (NEVER call them guns) on the range to determine our highest marksmanship levels. Throughout all of the training and routine, we learned to obey orders with out questioning. That could be life saving in combat.

With the constant routine of marching to classes with layers of clothing on, several men got sick with more than mere snuffles. In fact, in another company one man died of spinal meningitis, and then we all had to line up once a day for a supposedly preventative medicine. At one point, 'they' had us sit on the floor all around the edge of the Dayroom while attaching tubes to our arms to collect blood. I suppose it was for testing, but we had to sit there and wait for the blood to slowly fill a test tube. Some could barely sit up by the end of a half hour. In the fourth week, I became quite logy and groggy with upper respiratory problems and finally reported to sick call. With a temperature of 102 I was put in the hospital and given shots of penicillin. Now came the worry of getting out in time to avoid getting "recycled" to another company due to how much I missed. As it turned out, I just made the limit of days required and came back to my company in the middle of marksmanship training. I was glad to be back and didn't even mind that I was not topnotch because of not having prepared my rifle sights adequately. I passed the minimum level of accuracy required and breathed a sigh of relief.

During this eight weeks of Basic Training, we were not allowed to leave the Fort at all until the fourth week. Then I could get a pass to go to Albany for a weekend. Barbara and I got a chance to meet at her grandmother's house in East Orange, NJ, one weekend, which was a great boost to our morale. The main activity that saved my sanity in Fort Dix was singing. I had sung in church choir all four years of college and always liked being in a chorus. I learned that the Protestant Chaplain directed a chorus that anyone could join. We had weekly practice and went on the road to perform once or twice. This was a great distraction from the daily routine.

In March, the training ended and I would have a ten day leave before returning to duty. During the Fort Dix time, we took a written test to see if we qualified for Officers' Candidate School. I passed and was invited to do that, but found out it would add another year to my service, so I said "No, thank you." Then I was called in to discuss what else might be a direction for me. With a Bachelor's in Math and a Masters in Education, I thought they would find something. It was suggested that I might be interested in training in cartography. I have always liked maps and thought this would be a good fit, so I agreed and was given orders to report to Fort Bliss, Texas, after my leave.

During my eight weeks of the first half of Basic Training, all was not quiet with the Cold War. In February, the Baghdad Pact was signed by Iran, Iraq, Pakistan, Turkey, and the United Kingdom. Its purpose was to resist the spread of Communism in the Middle East. Then, in March, the Soviet Union began a program of aid to Syria. The two countries were allied throughout the Cold War.

Also in March, Barbara and I had a wonderful ten day interlude being together and seeing family and friends during my ten day leave. We even got up to Stowe, Vermont, for a few days of skiing and stayed in a really nice guest house, a former farm house now serving skiers family style. But, of course, this time came to an end, and I was off to Texas with the two of us planning how we could be together out there somehow. Again, we were naïve. But back I went to Fort Dix, turned in my field gear and flew to Texas, thinking that everything would work out somehow, although I was not making decisions for the Army.

CHAPTER FIVE

Things Are Not As "They" Said

Fort Bliss, Texas

March - May 1955

Everyone should know that the military does not always do what it says it will. Details somehow get lost in translation. My orders did not say that I was to report to Fort Bliss for cartography training. It said that I was reporting for "evaluation and assignment". So, along with many other college educated men, I was shoved into an anti-aircraft training unit (a battery instead of a company). There were lawyers, teachers and several other occupations represented in our battery that was housed in many four-man wooden huts that had been used for German prisoners of war. There was just enough space for each of us to have a corner area for bunk, footlocker and space for hanging uniforms.

Oh yes, and space for newly issued field gear like we had at Fort Dix. A single row of huts formed three sides of a 50 by 100 yard rectangle on slightly slanted land. The fourth side was occupied by a longer building housing our battery's headquarters. The latrine (complete with clothes washer) was a separate building up the row with the headquarters (Orderly Room), and the mess hall was farther up, at the top of the hill.

Every morning we stood at rigid attention for personal inspection, which included our shaving results and the cleanness of our combat boots. One particular sergeant took great fun in humiliating anyone without a close enough shave or dusty boots. I had persuaded myself to just follow that stuff and keep a low profile. However, those mornings were beautiful, with the rising sun turning the nearby, barren mountains into gorgeous bright red walls.

We learned the fine art of fifty caliber machine gun mechanics, as well as how to take it apart and put it together. We did the same with 40 millimeter cannons so that we could learn to shoot two of those mounted on an open turret tank and to shoot four of the machine guns simultaneously mounted on a half-track vehicle. We were all quick to learn and even got used to being badgered by cadre (non-commissioned officers doing the instruction), who were threatened by the amount of education standing before them. The food was excellent, the facilities bare and the Saturday stand-at-attention-in-the-sun formations tolerable. In those weekly formations I learned the meaning of existentialism, the idea that in any set of circumstances a person can always discover an option to help overcome hardship.

We were required to stand at rigid attention for stretches of time, neither moving nor changing facial expression. I found I could wiggle my knee caps without detection for as long as I wanted while still complying with orders. Even when under the control of other people, one can find an outlet. We still have choices.

So there we were, a mixed group of men with a range of ages and occupations. All of us had been sent for a specialty, but were instead assigned to Artillery training. The sergeants and corporals who ran the training were hard on us and prone to make fun of our education. Every day, while we were at training activities, they inspected our huts and messed up beds that were not neat and tightly made. I decided to be a wall flower, not drawing attention and just getting through all of that. There were other men of my 23 year age and some older, since Selective Service could draft a person up to age 26. There wasn't much in the form of leisure activities, but we could get day passes and go in to El Paso or Juarez, Mexico. No overnights were allowed. I did get to spend some time with my former college roommate and his wife and baby in El Paso. He was assigned to Fort Bliss for the rest of his time in service. I also went with some of the guys to a bullfight in Juarez. We sat on the sunny side for cheaper tickets and shared a bottle of tequila. One of the guys was wide-eyed when he realized that the matador really would kill the bull, so we passed him the bottle more often.

Late in this Advanced Basic Training, our battery went to the desert of White Sands, New Mexico, for live weapon firing. We lived in pup tents and spent the time either firing or cleaning the guns. Once or twice we were hit by big sand storms. Activity was cancelled, and we hid in our tents until they ended, coming out at the end with sand smeared faces and guns needing major cleaning. At least once, I went through the chow line with my mess kit in hand and watched the food on it turn brown. One time the vanilla ice cream became chocolate looking, and the whole meal had to be dumped. As we cleaned our mess kits in barrels of sudsy water, I wondered why the sergeants were on our backs to rinse the kits thoroughly. It wasn't because of leftover food being stuck to them. It was that they were worried we wouldn't rinse out the soap well enough to prevent stomach problems later.

We fired our weapons live at a large mesh banner towed by a small remote-controlled plane. The big excitement happened one day when someone in another battery mistakenly hit the plane instead of what it was dragging. Oops.

During this 8 weeks of training, I turned 24 on April 12. In national news, it was announced that day that Dr. Jonas Salk had successfully developed a vaccine to prevent polio. Also in April, an international organization of states was formed, named the Non-Aligned Movement, pioneered by Nehru of India, Sukarno of Indonesia, Tito of Yugoslavia, Nasser of Egypt and Nkrumah of Ghana. Their aim was to head off polarization of the world and give more voice to smaller nations. They were not formally aligned with or against any of the major powers of that time.

In May, West Germany joined NATO and began rearmament. The Warsaw Pact was established in Eastern Europe to be a Communist counterpart to NATO. The countries involved were East Germany, Czechoslovakia, Poland, Hungary, Romania, Albania, Bulgaria and the Soviet Union. At the same time, Austria became a neutral country and its occupation by the Allies ended.

Barbara had talked about driving west to Texas alone, which I thought not to be a good idea, for several reasons, but I liked her willingness to do something about our distance apart. It turned out to be impossible when we learned that she was pregnant. I was missing her terribly, but there was nothing to do about it. At that time a new love song, "Unchained Melody" became popular, so I adopted it to help get through this. It didn't stay in the public eye (or ear) then, but became popular 50 years later as the theme song for the movie "Ghost". Even today, I get emotional when I hear the words "Oh, my love, my darling I've hungered for your touch a long lonely time." especially now that I am widowed.

After returning to Fort Bliss, we soldiers finished our training and waited to learn of our assignments that would locate each of us for the duration of our "hitch" in the Army. It turned out that we were divided into four groups. One would go to Korea, one would go to Fort Benning, Georgia, one would go to Fort Gordon, Georgia, and the fourth, which included me, would go to West Germany.

I thought that was terrible and the end of our personal planning for Barbara to be with me. Then, I was approached by a young soldier who was frightened about going to Georgia, because of being black in the mid-fifties in the South. He wondered if we could swap assignments. I readily agreed to give it a try, but we were told the orders could not be changed. I have often wondered how he made out.

So by then it was late May, and we were all getting ready to be moved. My group was scheduled to fly to New Jersey and be located at Camp Kilmer, a small base used for transit of troops. For some reason, I was assigned to be the leader of my group and be responsible for the boxes of our military records. I had kept a low profile the whole time, but maybe I was chosen for being older and married. Sergeant Chavez, who was always putting us down for the smallest reason, came up to me and said he didn't know I was a math teacher in civilian life. He said that maybe I could have helped him with math, if he had found out sooner. Too late, but it might not have worked anyway.

We flew from Biggs Army Air Base all night to New Jersey (no jets) in our winter uniforms, because it wasn't Memorial Day yet and rules said uniforms went by the calendar, not by the weather. It was OK in dry old Texas, but when we came down the stairs at Maguire Air Base, carrying our heavy duffel bags, we were dripping with sweat by the time we got to the bottom.

A bus took us to Kilmer, and we were assigned to one-story barracks. We were there about ten days, moving furniture so they could close the base, while we waited for the next leg of the trip.

Actually, Kilmer was reopened a year later for Hungarian refugees of that uprising.

Another older draftee and I decided to work up a church service for the Sunday we were there, using the seemingly deserted chapel. He was a 26 year-old lawyer, very bright, but not strong. We had become good friends. He had had a really rough time with calisthenics at Fort Bliss. We thought volunteering to present a worship service would be a worthwhile project. I played the organ and led the singing while he did the praying and preaching. We made a good pair.

Next stop was a troop ship at the Brooklyn Navy Yard.

CHAPTER SIX

To West Germany And More Surprises

In Transit

June 1955

Life aboard a troop ship was definitely a new experience. Once on board, I was assigned to the middle of three stacked bunks with space for my duffel bag, but that was all. I was assigned the job of baking for the voyage to Bremerhaven, West Germany. My daily shift was 9:00 PM to 3:00 AM, which came with a special tag for my bunk that said I could sleep through morning inspections. The number of hours in each shift was reduced as we traveled east and changed time zones at night. So I stirred huge batches of pie filling of all flavors and then spread it on large sheets of dough in equally large trays by night and relaxed on deck by day in the warm June weather. Later I found out that Army bakers on board were serving guard duty while I did their kind of work.

Nine days later we docked at Bremerhaven. My group was herded onto a train for a half-day ride to Zwiebrucken (two bridges) just over the border from northeastern France. There the US Army maintained a base for sorting out new arrivals and assigning them to units throughout West Germany. We were surprised to be told that artillery personnel were not needed at this time. What next?

What the Army needed was more tankers to help the outfits that were guarding the Czechoslovakian border. Consequently, we were assigned to the 6th Armored Cavalry Regiment in the state of Bavaria in the southwest corner of West Germany. This meant another train ride which took most of the day, but was actually rewarding in terms of seeing the countryside and the people. The train would stop briefly in various towns and cities, and I watched school children wearing backpacks heading home. As we passed through Nuremburg we saw results of the WW2 bombing raids. The roof of the railroad station was completely gone - wide open to the sky.

Our group was split up over the three battalions of the Regiment and located at Regensburg, Landshut and Passau. Regimental Headquarters was in Straubing. On the train ride I had been wondering, "What in hell is an armored cavalry?" since Armored implies tanks and Cavalry implies horses and I knew that the Army no longer had horses.

The answer was a mechanized outfit with jeeps, halftracks, personnel carriers, trucks, trailers and, of course, tanks. Unlike the Infantry, every man was assigned to a vehicle. Each battalion consisted of three combat companies and a battalion headquarters company. A company consisted of three combat platoons of 8-10 men each and a headquarters platoon of specialists such as the Armorer, the Company Clerk, the Supply Clerk the vehicles mechanic, and the Communications man. At that time I didn't care about the history of the Regiment, but I have since learned about it through the internet. The 6th Armored Calvary was part of the 4th Army during World War II and took part in D-Day and the Battle of the Bulge. Afterward, it stayed in West Germany to patrol 172 miles of the German-Czech border and to assist with the reconstruction of Germany. The Bavarian Government was so thankful for the Regiment's help that it presented it with the Shield of Bavaria, now on display in the Regiment's museum, the only known official recognition of an American unit by a German State.

I was assigned to the third platoon of I Company in Regensburg, issued another set of field gear, and shared a two-man room on the first floor with a younger guy who had been drafted in that original group from Worcester, Massachusetts, that I met at the Albany Draft Board. He had been in the same Basic Training groups along the way to this point. We got along well. Oh, I forgot to mention that I had become a tank gunner after all of this assigning.

The barracks were very unique, to my thinking. Two-man rooms and a marble floored bath down the hall. These were former Nazi barracks housing 4 companies - G, H, I and Headquarters. It was really one long, two-story building looking like a series of the letter U all joined at the sides. Each company had its own dayroom, mess hall and company office. The mess hall was a separate building behind our quarters on the same level as the basement and operated by German nationals. The supply rooms and the Armory were also on the basement level of the main building for each company. In addition, the motor pool and base housing for officers and non-commissioned officers (non-coms) completed the Fort area.

The Third Battalion base was named Fort Skelly. When entering the Fort and passing through the guarded gatehouse, there was a battalion headquarters building and a long building that housed the USO Club and an auditorium used as a chapel or a movie theater. All buildings were tile roofed with stucco siding.

Headquarters building on left, Snack bar, USO
room, theater/chapel on the right

Away from Fort Skelly, but walkable, were the PX (Post
Exchange), Quartermaster laundry and gas station, and, separately,
a hospital and quarters for Army nurses, all located on a wide avenue
named Landshutter Strasse (meaning the road to Landshut), which
also showed signs of damage from bombing and machine gun fire. In
other words, the total base was divided among three installations. The
city itself was founded by the Romans in the 9th century on the banks
of the Danube River. It was heavily bombed because of the presence
of its Messerschmitt fighter plane factory and an oil refinery, but the
spires of the Gothic cathedral and the ancient stone bridge over the
Danube were spared. The 12th C. bridge is on the front cover.

After we had arrived and settled in, we were issued field gear,
as at Ft. Dix, and a weapon. The latter was a 30 caliber carbine
kept locked up in the Armory when not needed. We quickly had the
correct patches sewn on our clothing to indicate the 6th Armored

Calvary (an orange unicorn on a blue field) on the left breast pocket and the 7th US Army (a gold capital A with 7 steps up each oblique side representing "7 steps to hell", its motto), on the left shoulder. Being Privates, we had no insignia of rank to go on the upper sleeves. Our names were already on our uniforms over the right breast pocket.

Within a few days of all that, our company and the rest of the battalion "moved out" to participate in maneuvers (combat practice) with the Regiment. This meant loading every vehicle on railroad flatcars to travel to the appointed place. We rode in passenger cars. I must mention here, that at this point I had no instruction or familiarization with my new role as a tank gunner. In short, I didn't know the insides of an enclosed turret or how to operate one or how the gun was aimed through a small window and then fired. I will come back to that later, so the reader has now had fair warning.

When we reached the "battle" location and unloaded the vehicles, our company was assigned a site. My tank sergeant, Sgt. Nevins, was told our spot, and we positioned our tank there. Because West Germany was by then a sovereign nation, we could not dig foxholes in the land allotted to the Army for practicing mock warfare. Instead, each soldier laid out a perimeter of a foxhole using yellow tape. The Regiment had also had to put rubber pads between the treads on the tanks.

Being on a tank was not what I had envisioned where I would be after basic, but it could have been worse. One advantage of riding on a tank when the Battalion went into the woods on maneuvers was that we could heat our canned C-rations by laying the cans on the rear deck next to the manifold (hotter than the muffler) to heat. They would be just right when the column of vehicles stopped for a break.

The next day, during a time that didn't require me to do an assigned task, I sat in my tank to find my way around. I would have thought that I would have been previously sent to another tank gunner before leaving Fort Skelly to be shown how to operate the equipment. I knew that the tank crew included a commander, a driver, a loader and a gunner. As I sat there in thought, I studied each switch or lever on the gunner's instrument panel. When I gently touched one small lever, there was an immediate explosion as my cannon roared. Then all hell broke loose outside the tank, so I stayed hidden inside it. The company commander chewed out my tank commander, as I had inadvertently knocked out G Company. Sgt. Nevins was ordered to punish me, but he later said it wasn't my fault that I wasn't instructed ahead of time. Thank God it was a dummy shell! I, of course, received good natured jibes from my fellow GI's for several weeks after.

CHAPTER SEVEN

A New Job

Summer 1955

With the exception of one practice alert, which only lasted through the day, Company I stayed on base during the month of July. The men took care of their vehicles and gear, trained and took turns in small groups pulling guard duty from 4:00 PM to 8:00 AM. I learned more about my tank's cannon, of course, and felt more confident in my duties therein. Most of the guys went out drinking for entertainment, but I focused on movies or using the facilities of the darkroom at the USO club and of course wrote letters home. Barbara was making plans to come overseas now that I was permanently stationed.

All of my group of June arrivals were becoming accustomed to the routine, the countryside and the money. At that time the currency exchange was four Deutsche Marks to the Dollar. Therefore, our enlisted men's pay went a long way in purchases, beer and restaurants. We were paid in cash in dollars, but it was in special script bills, including change. Pennies were the only American coins, which took some adapting on our part. The GIs all referred to the US as "the land where nickels clink." Soldiers could set up bank accounts at American

Express which had an office near the Army's off base facilities, which was convenient. Barbara received a separate dependent's allotment.

Our Regiment manned two sectors of the Czech/Bavaria border, utilizing two base Camps which reminded me of Boy Scout camps. It was an area like the New York Adirondacks - pine forests and low mountains. The companies took turns moving up to the camps two at a time for about 10 days. From there, platoons took turns on watch with 50 caliber machine guns pointed at the actual border. Our company did not draw that duty that month.

The Cold War was fairly calm at that time. The only world event was a meeting in mid-July of President Eisenhower, Prime Minister Anthony Eden of the United Kingdom, Premier Nikolai Bulganin of the Soviet Union and Prime Minister Edgar Faure of France, now referred to as "The Big Four", in Geneva, Switzerland.

One early morning in August (5:00 AM), some of the companies of the 6th Armored Cavalry packed up and moved north by train to camp as standby units during the interchange of two Armored Cavalry regiments. On the way, I put an old Army adage to use - sleep when you can because you don't know when you will get the next chance. I was in a third class compartment with other men and very tired, so I climbed up into the overhead luggage rack, draped my body across its metal partition and slept well.

One regiment had been guarding the East German border and was rotating back to the United States. Another regiment was coming over to take their place, and backup was necessary as a precaution. We didn't have many duties, but it wasn't a vacation either. Evenings I worked with my tank commander, helping him with spelling. He had been promoted on the battlefields of Korea and wanted to improve his language skills. Most of the time it rained, and we were in a huge tent with a grass floor, not adding to morale. However, we did get to go to a country fair one night, complete with huge beer drinking tent and a scary roller coaster with each person in a solo car.

Each company in the Battalion was staffed by a 1st Lieutenant or Captain as commander, an Executive Officer and three Lieutenants. Each of the latter commanded a platoon and held other company duties. One day, Lieutenant Wynan, who was our Education Officer, came from the company office (a smaller tent) into the barracks tent and called my name. When I reported to him, he said that he noted from my records that I could type. I said "Yes, Sir". He asked me how fast. I stretched the truth a little by saying 50 words a minute. I had taken business typing in high school, and I could type fast then, so why not now.

He asked if I would like to become the Company Clerk, as ours was finishing his tour of duty and going home. I, of course, said "Yes, Sir." I could not believe that with two college degrees, a year of high school typing was going to get me off of a tank! He told me about the situation and said the change would happen very soon. At the same time, our Company Commander was leaving, too. Before my change occurred, things changed. The departing commander had needed a Clerk who spoke German, but the arriving officer spoke German, so another PFC became the new Clerk and I became the Company's Supply Clerk. I was also a Private First Class (PFC) by then.

The Company Clerk's duties included clerical duties, correspondence, keeping the daily roster and driving the Company Commander. The Supply Clerk's job was, back at home base, not under the constant eye of the officers and was located, as previously mentioned, down in the ground level. It included a lot of typing of orders for supplies and reports, as well as keeping Debit and Credit account books on all equipment issued to the company. That last included every piece of field gear and every tool in the Motor Pool, down to the smallest screwdriver, as well as every vehicle. I learned quickly how to answer the phone military style. "Company I Supply PFC Conroe Sir."The "Sir" was very important because you never knew the rank of the person calling. We also had to keep checking our spare materials on the shelves of the Supply Room and have all in order whenever Battalion or Regiment headquarters sent a senior officer to inspect our operation.

As soon as we returned to Fort Skelly, I was on duty in the Supply Room, working under the Supply Sergeant, SFC Edmonds. I was also relocated in the barracks from the 3rd Platoon living area to the headquarters platoon quarters, a large room housing the Company Clerk, the Communications man and myself. The Armorer, Cpl. Harrison, lived off base with his wife as did the main auto mechanic, Sgt. Hendrix.

I learned the job fairly quickly and my typing speed returned rapidly. I should mention that this was before electric typewriters. Mine was an excellent German typewriter, but with no copy machines yet, either, requisitions had to be typed with 6 carbon copies. For young readers, I should explain that "carbon copies" were attained by adding 6 sheets of typing paper alternating with 6 sheets of carbon paper, plain on one side and inky on the other side that faced the next page. This required erasing any typing error on each of the six sheets while moving the total 13 sheets manually by turning the roller in the carriage of the typewriter.

Meanwhile, plans were going ahead for Barbara to come across the Atlantic. She had booked passage for September 3rd on Swedish-American Line's Stockholm. With what few German phrases I had picked up, I went searching for a place to live. It had to be close to the Fort, because we wouldn't have a car for a while, and it had to have a phone connection, so that I could be called when the monthly alert occurred. This was not an easy task, because there weren't apartment houses near the Fort, so I had to go house to house and ask if they had rooms to rent in my limited German. It was a daunting task, but, I was young, determined and very much in love.

CHAPTER EIGHT

A Home Is Found

September 1955

So, I went on searching and it helped to talk with other GI couples living off base. The Harrisons and the Hendrixes, for example, lived near Fort Skelly. Originally, I had thought it not a good place for Barbara to come to, but she had persevered in convincing me that we could handle whatever was needed. She was fiercely determined that she would come so that I would not miss the first year of my first-born's life. It's hard to argue with a pregnant woman when she has your interest at heart.

As previously mentioned, the Stockholm sailed from Manhattan on September 3, two days after Barbara's 24th birthday. The families gathered for the sendoff in New York. My parents, Barbara's parents and brother, Gordon, and her Aunt Agnes Holme, plus her cousin, his wife and small daughter all met and talked together on the boat's deck. In those days, this was common practice. There were no fears of terrorism, and some people even entertained their friends. The visitors were all ushered down the boarding ramp, which was then hauled away, and music and decorative paper streamers celebrated the event. Too bad that we have had to give up that pleasure.

I had accrued leave time, so was able to arrange time off to go to Bremerhaven on the north coast to meet Barb's ship. Of course, I had a set of Army orders to cover my leave. That was required with every leave-taking, but not for traveling on your own on a national holiday. Anyway, off I went, arriving at the dockyard on a dismal, clouded day and watched the white ship with its ice breaking bow ease into its dock. what a thrill it was to see her looking down from the deck rail. Five fee two with curly hair and blue eyes never looked so good to me, even with the bulge in her midsection. I hardly remember the details of how we arranged for her steamer trunk to be shipped from the SS Stockholm or where we stayed.

The trip back south was nice because we had that time to ourselves and much to talk about. Barbara described her trip on the Stockholm to me. She became good friends with another young Army wife on her way to join her husband in West Germany. She said that going around the British Isles north of Scotland was really dramatic. She noted that there were people on board who had fled Germany and were now going back. One man told Barbara that he was going back to Germany to search for family members, if any were still alive. That was sobering.

The Stockholm is here. Barb is under
the left lifeboat 4th from right.

Back in Regensburg, we checked in to the Maximilian Hotel downtown. It was great and it took us no time at all to get used to the fat comforters on the bed. The better to snuggle with. Barbara hung out there while I searched for a place to live. One day, when I came back to the hotel, she was laughing away at herself. It seems that it is difficult for a medium sized, 6-months pregnant woman to get up out of huge old bathtubs. To help herself, she pulled on a convenient cord hanging from the ceiling. It got her out OK, but it called the maid as well! Did we ever laugh!

We moved into the second floor of a small house of a family of four. They rented us what was really a bedroom with the promise of finishing a second one. The two rooms were separated by attic space. That was where we kept food that needed refrigeration and parked Barbara's steamer trunk.

A word about the trunk. It was at least 3 1/2 feet tall and opened into two halves. One half was for hanging clothes, and other half had drawers like a dresser. It was sort of an instant closet and dresser. During the first half of the 20th Century, people traveled like that on long cruises to have enough clothes - formal and informal. Wash and wear hadn't been invented yet.

The dead end street was dirt but very near the Fort. It was the same street as our friends, Hinterher Muhlweg (outlying mill way) with small houses each with a fenced yard and locked gate. The Roche family crowded into their first floor, but I could tell that they needed the money, because the first floor consisted of only two large rooms and a large hall.

We bought a 2-burner hotplate and arranged for my supply truck driver, Cpl. Steele, to bring Barb's big trunk and two army cots plus sheets and blankets to our tiny abode. A small cupboard, a table, 2 chairs and a wardrobe completed the furnishings. Oh yes, and a small coal stove was there for heat. The Roches had had pipes and a sink installed for water - cold only.

Then I was back in the Supply Room at work. In the end of September, we had to go to Munich to have Barb's passport stamped for permanent residence. We took the train south for that task and were surprised to step off the train to find huge barrels of beer on the Munich platform. It was Oktoberfest! Everyone could fill a glass or mug and pay at a counter. Neat!

Heading into October, we were preparing for our new arrival. We had no car, so walked to the Strassenbahn stop to ride downtown to buy equipment. On one trip we bought a changing table/baby bath and, on another trip, a carriage (Kinder wagon), but couldn't get that on the tram, so we walked the whole way home, pushing an empty carriage. What fun. I pushed it crazily at one point, causing stares and glares from proper Bavarians until they looked in and found it empty. Barbara's winter coat hid her bulge. These crazy Americans!

Our room shaped up with a v-shaped clothes line dividing it into thirds - living, dining, cooking. By then, the landlord had finished another room for our bedroom. The not-so-out house was downstairs inside the front door. We had three keys - one to the gate, one for the front door and one for our door. The other American couples on our street had the same. We had cold water to our room, running in but not out. Herr Roche said the drain would be finished next year when "haben mehr Gelt" (having more money, all German nouns are capitalized). So every noon when I walked in for lunch, I carried out a pail of wash water. We never did get a drain before we moved to a better situation.

The family was nice. The teenage boy and girl spoke English and we learned a little German. Barbara, being home all day learned from the Frau, who was sort of a natural teacher. She was very kind. Herr had a chip on his shoulder, however. I think it was from the war and the lack of more money. He often prodded me for cigarettes, which I willing gave if that would improve our situation.

Down the street there was a small grocery shop. Herr Pohl's phone was our only communication. That was how the company could call us for a practice alert. It was actually a pleasant life. We could go to movies on base and the assembly hall used for that became a Catholic chapel for one hour on Sunday morning and a Protestant chapel for the next hour. We even joined a Protestant group of both officers and enlisted people for a Bible study group.

A major problem was our lack of bathing facilities. It was easier for me as I could take a shower over at the Company quarters. Barbara walked to the Kaserne (barracks yard) that held the hospital and showered in the nurses' quarters. We seemed to get by with all of the inconvenience without complaining, because we were together, and that was so important. And our cash flow had improved with an off-base housing allowance, and, with the exchange rate so good, we were OK. In fact better off on PFC's pay than if I had gone to Georgia from Fort Bliss.

We learned a bit about managing coal stoves. Ours was tiny, not really heating up the room well. Coal came in two sizes - bricks and egg shaped coal (Eirkohlen) like we use today in grills. You start with paper and wood, add a few lumps of coal and then a brick. The bricks put out a nice heat and lasted a few hours, so the stove could be ignored for awhile.

We developed a very pleasant routine, managing the stove, cooking on two burners, taking walks, and, of course, I went to work each weekday and came home to lunch. We were a little startled the first time we heard an outboard motor boat coming down our little street. We rushed to the front window in search of it. It was instead a new automotive creation that sounded like an outboard motor. The Mescherschmitt factory was heavily bombed during the war and was now producing tiny 3-wheeled cars, big enough for two people sitting in tandem. The third wheel was on the rear and did the steering. The whole thing looked like a fighter plane cockpit mounted on wheels. Very inventive of them and economical to drive, I bet.

We were very fortunate that one of the younger sergeants in my company and his wife became our friends. They and their children lived on base and were generous with their time, taking us on drives into the countryside on occasional weekends. A year later he became my boss. We attended church services at the base chapel, where your military rank didn't matter, and that added a lot to our feeling that we had new friends.

Meanwhile, I was, of course, at the Supply Room every day. Barbara didn't mind being home and thoroughly enjoyed our landlady. Housework was not difficult, except for washing clothes. Mine went to Quartermaster Laundry. I was also called upon, as were all enlisted personnel, for guard duty at night. Rosters were posted, and we had to show up at Battalion headquarters in dress uniform with our assigned weapons. The group would be divided into shifts, and every four hours through the night the incoming shift was marched around to the guard posts with those coming off marching back to the guard room for naps.

However, this arrangement could work havoc with our Supply Room routine, as I would have to be at the guardhouse by 4:00 PM, regardless of what was still undone. This reached a head in my favor. One day I had to leave the office at 3:00 to go home and get ready for guard duty. Some requisitions needed to be typed to go to Battalion, and I was out of time. These had to be typed with the required 6 copies using carbon paper, which is terrible when you have to correct a typo. Sergeant Edmonds was quite angry about the situation and pulled strings somewhere the next day. That was the last time I was called for guard duty.

We were all glad that the world scene was pretty calm then as we approached Thanksgiving. That was a very nice day. Those of us living off base could bring our wives to the mess hall for a nice turkey dinner. By now, it was getting close to December, and Barbara's due date was the 12th. Time to get serious about this baby business. She had been going to the Army doctor regularly, and we also knew him and his wife in the Bible group. They told us to phone ahead for an Army ambulance when she went into labor.

However (and there's always a however), we had previously been told that first babies could not be delivered in the relatively small

Army hospital in Regensburg. For a first baby, Barb would have to go to Munich and wait in a hotel. Then the Army changed its mind and said first babies could be born in Regensburg if x-rays were taken first in Munich to forestall difficulties. Barb went by train to Munich by herself and had the x-rays like a real trooper. BUT the x-rays did not get to Regensburg before the baby came!

My Company Commander was an experienced and confident soldier. He didn't strike me as very compassionate, but he surprised me. The company was moving out for winter maneuvers, and he called me to his office to tell me that with our baby due soon I was to stay back. I was really grateful and Barbara was much relieved.

The company left on a Tuesday, and the doctor told Barbara "no more salt". So, on the morning of the next day which was December 7th (Pearl Harbor Day), the alarm went off at 6:30 as usual. I awoke to discover that Barbara was starting labor. I quickly shaved, ate and dressed before rushing down the street to the phone. In about 15 minutes the ambulance arrived and off we went, rattling along our dirt road as the overnight hoar frost was beginning to melt. By 10:00, I was told it would be a long while, being the first baby, and I should go to work. I went up to see Barb first and found her fairly jumping around the bed, so I didn't leave. Scott Alan was born at 1:30 with all appendages and close to 7 pounds. I worried about his pointed head, but was assured it was normal and would change to a proper shape. That had started by the next day. Our landlords were very thrilled that the hog they were raising for food had gone to the butcher at 6 AM and Barb had gone to the hospital at 8. What a day to celebrate.

I was on top of the world and went immediately to American Express to send a telegram to Barb's parents and buy cigars. How exciting it was!! When the company returned on Thursday, I stood in the Company office and handed out cigars, receiving happy congratulations. I was very proud of my new son and his mother, Frau Barbara, as the Roche family called her.

The medical people kept mother and son in the hospital extra days because of our living conditions, so they came home on Saturday, after I settled the hospital bill of $10.50. That was for Barbara's food.

Now we had real "room dividers" in our quarters - wet diapers. We had to heat water on the hot plate to wash them, but they did separate the 3 parts of the room admirably, with Scotty sleeping in his Kinderwagon in the middle section. Oh, to have our brand new automatic washer with us instead of its sitting in Barb's parents' basement!

Christmas was shortly on the way by now. Frau Roche began baking cookies and filled three suitcases that she guarded under her bed. We sent home cards and small presents, but, otherwise did not have much preparation. Especially since we would go to I Company Mess for Christmas dinner.

The Roches decorated downstairs, with father and daughter arguing over the Christmas tree. At one point, explosive Herr Roche threatened to hit her in the head with the butt of the tree trunk. I stuck my nose in to see what all of the noise was about, and that cooled things.

On Christmas Eve, the Roches celebrated with cookies and presents to each other. The naturally grown tree was ablaze with real candles. A spectacular sight, but a little dicey. Dinner on base was very nice.

Altogether quite a year had passed. At the end of it, the West German government announced that 271 East German refugees had crossed into West Germany that year to get away from the communist state.

Little did we know how tense and mind boggling 1956 would be for us and the world.

CHAPTER NINE

The New Year Begins - 1956

January was a time of our streamlining our routine. We had learned a lot already about cloth diapers, breast feeding and coal stoves. A little snow had arrived, but so had the cold temperatures. Years later, while on a tour in southern France, our guide mentioned that 1956 was the coldest year in Europe in the 20th Century. No wonder our little stove required constant attention.

The world scene was fairly quiet that month, giving everyone a good feeling about the 6th Armored Cavalry's job at the Czech border. Little did we know, thank goodness, how tense everything was going to get as the year wore on.

We discovered we could take Scotty with us down the street to the Hendrix's so the adults could play cards, laying him out on their bed to sleep. It was also easy to take him with us to the movies on base, and he would sleep on my lap.

This month, we had to take another train trip to Munich to get Scotty some legality. The Army hospital had already given us papers titled "Report of Child born Abroad of American Parents". However, we discovered that we needed a copy of my birth certificate with a raised seal, since I had no passport. We had a photocopy of my birth certificate, but had to write to my parents for a copy with raised seal. My father went to Bath, New York, in the western New York's Steuben County wherein I was born and obtained the needed copy. That was then mailed to us. We took these papers, plus Barbara's passport and a close up photo of the month old, plus the one month old himself, with us. The first was for proof so he could have US citizenship and the photo to be added to Barbara's passport. US troops in Europe did not need passports.

Before or right after that trip, I visited Regensburg's Standesampt (Registration Office) to get a German birth certificate for him in several copies. Now that was an experience right out of a Charles Dickens novel, "A Christmas Carol", I think. I could see Bob Cratchet toiling at an ancient desk with quill pen to dip in ink and a blotter to dry it.

A very polite, older gentleman helped me and made seven copies, each completed manually and dried with a semi-circular blotter that rolled back and forth. Also, each copy had special stamps affixed to it to make it official. I couldn't see us returning in the far future for copies, so seven was just right.

February became difficult at the outset. The temperatures got worse, and the East Germans deliberately held back supplies of coal. We didn't use the new bedroom in our lodgings, which would have required tending a second coal stove. Barbara and I slept head to toe in the Army cot that served as our sofa. Scotty was fine in his carriage in the middle of the floor. It had a tubular, collapsible frame and chrome fenders. The bed part lifted out and could be collapsed, too. He was plenty warm inside it, with its solid fabric sides.

Then we realized that the walls of our room were coated with about ¼ inch of ice. Sgt. Edmonds and his wife insisted we stay with them in base housing for awhile. That was a life saver, but we needed to move to another place.

Father and son "reading" the Stars and Stripes

Rather quickly, I found a place for us even nearer the Fort. A German family had built a Gasthaus (pub) after World War II, one floor at a time. It was finished with a small living space in the cellar, the pub on the first floor, and two floors of the family's living space above. The pub had rest rooms with real plumbing, as did the modern bathroom upstairs.

We moved, with the help of the supply truck, into the basement space. One large room with a cooking coal stove, complete with an oven. We also had the use of the space outside our room for Barbara's steamer trunk (acting as a closet and dresser), and a place to sit. We even were allotted half of the ice box that chilled the beer. Excellent, since we had had no refrigeration at the Roches'.

The room had twin beds, a wardrobe, a chest of drawers and a dining table with chairs. We laughed when we discovered that the men playing cards upstairs on a Saturday night

Number 59 Unterischlinger Weg

thumped the cards on their table as they played. There were other perks, too. I could buy ½ liter bottles of beer for 50 pfennigs (12 ½ cents). One hundred pfennigs equal one Mark. The pub also had a phone, handy for alerts, and the motor pool was diagonally across the street, which was named Unterislinger Weg (the way to Unterisling).

In the back yard there was a long building housing a laundry room and a two room apartment where a very young American couple lived. Every Saturday the Schreiders fired up the water heater to wash clothes and our sheets. They also fired up the water heater in their bathroom, and Barbara could take a real bath there if she so desired. Nice!! Oh, AND the family had three young girls, one of whom was old enough to baby sit. Frau Schreider ran the Gasthaus, while her husband and older sons ran a mobile canteen serving food to construction workers. The industrious Germans were rebuilding.

I should also mention that they lost a son at the close of the war for lack of medicine.

We were much warmer now and had a much better situation. We were closer to Fort Skelly, but farther from the other two parts (Kasernes) of the installation. Walking to the PX for groceries was a bit of a haul, but we could also use local groceries. We didn't mind walking at all. It was especially nice when one or more of Regensburg's churches had its bells ringing. Every day there would be bells exercising somewhere, and it made a wonderful atmosphere. At about this time, it dawned on us that Barbara's naturally curly hair had returned to its natural self. It went straight during the permanency. We didn't realize that this would also happen with future pregnancies. Not serious, but interesting.

Barbara and Scotty in our second housing

Our cooking facilities at housing #2. Sink
and ice box were outside the door.

A pleasant diversion from the world tensions came in the form of
the 1956 Winter Olympics, held in Cortina, Italy.

As February ended, the only Cold War incident of note was a
speech Nikita Khrushchev gave in Moscow. The title was "On the
Personality Cult and its Consequences", by which he launched De-
Stalinization. We were glad to know that the influence of that terrible
man was waning. However, we didn't assume that all was well with
the Kremlin and our country's relations with it.

CHAPTER TEN

Springtime And A Car

By the middle of March, the daylight hours were beginning to lengthen and the bitter cold had abated. We ventured downtown to our same baby equipment store to buy a crib. Our room was really larger than at the Roches, and we had space for it. Scotty was getting too big to sleep in the carriage.

The world was staying fairly calm, and our life drifted along normally. In April, we had a chance to buy a car from a soldier whose enlistment was up. This was common practice, passing furniture and cars along to others. The car was a two-door 1937 Opel that had obviously survived the war. It was gray in color and had turn signals that the GIs called "maax nix sticks." They popped up when turned on, and, among the German drivers, no one could tell if they were really going to turn. "It doesn't matter" translated to maax nix.

Now we could travel around Regensburg, admiring the ancient buildings and statues. We loved the ringing of church bells every day, and the history of the city. We bought a secondhand car seat that could also be a car bed. And back at "our" store, we bought a highchair made of wood with hinges halfway up two of the legs. We could fold the bottom of the legs that had a sizeable board attached between them up to the seat, and it became a play table. Neat!.

Easter was another spirit raiser. We needed one after some of the off base husbands and I were royally chewed out for almost missing an alert. We were threatened with having to move back on base and send our families home if it happened again. That's when I knew that Army life was not for us. I hated having higher ranking officers having control over my family. I never missed or was late to another alert, though. I also coached our landlady on the need for waking me up whenever the call came.

Easter Sunday was a beautiful day. We invited the Harrisons from our former street to come for roast chicken dinner. They were Catholic and went to Chapel first and then came and sat with Scotty and the roasting chicken while we went to the Protestant service. Dinner was very nice except for an accident. Barb had baked a cherry pie for the occasion. At desert time we hovered over our guests and pulled the pie from the warm oven. One of us held it while the other tried to remove the potholder that was stuck to the bottom of the pan. The other of us yanked at it, and the pie went upside down into the coal basket. Very sad, but we did laugh.

For my 25th birthday, Barbara ventured forth into downtown Regensburg with Frau Schreider to look for a hatchet for me. The better to split kindling wood with, you know. Downtown shops were all specialized in goods for sale. She had learned ahead that the correct word for hatchet was Hackel, but in her haste upon entering the shop, she blurted out "I need a Hackel" to the non-English speaking sales person, instead of learning the German. They all had a good laugh, and Barb did find a fine hatchet.

In May, I was promoted to the equivalent of Corporal. The Army had just changed things, though. Corporals were considered non-commissioned officers because they commanded men of lower ranks. Those of equal time in grade (the main basis for promotion) who did not command others were Specialists of various grades. I became a Specialist 3rd Class. It meant more pay and a good feeling to have advanced. As we drove around the ancient city, our little car fit right in with the traffic. Some officers and non-coms had brought American cars over, and these had difficulty turning corners on the narrow streets. We became quite adept at handling the streets. We had both been required to take driving tests for a special license.

We found that, with the advantageous exchange rate, we were able to go out to dinner sometimes. Our favorite spot was the Rathauskeller - literally the Rathaus (city hall) cellar and commonly called rathskeller by Americans. It dated back hundreds of years. We would get a table against the wall with a bench on that side. Scotty's car seat could sit on the bench with the table pushed up to him. He could chew on Bavarian rolls while we sampled wine and roast duck. It often cost about 10 Marks - $2.50.

However, the German civilian economy was not prepared for babies traveling. No highchairs in restaurants or cribs in hotels. And no baby food. Luckily we had the American PX for Gerbers Baby Food. At one point I had a heated argument with one of my company's sergeants about the use of the PX. He took the position that only Sergeants and above should be allowed to buy their food there. He was very biased and full of his rank. I argued that what were our children to eat, then, if we couldn't buy what we needed in the PX. The argument was a draw and didn't change our status.

Over Memorial Day weekend, we ventured forth on a trip to Ulm, farther up the Danube River, to visit a high school friend and his wife stationed there. We stopped one night at a hotel in Augsburg and then on to our hotel in Ulm. We took the car seat/bed into the hotels.

While in Ulm, we enjoyed catching up with our friends. We also toured the city with them and saw the gravesite of General Rommel.

After a successful career leading Nazi troops in North Africa, he tried to advise Hitler of French coast defenses and fell before Hitler's legendary rages. He was forced to take poison to avoid being labeled a traitor.

On the return trip, we admired the Bavarian scenery and watched for May poles in villages and stork nests on rooftops along the way. There were also fields of hops growing to be used in the beer making industry.

By June, a few unsettling events showed us that not all was quiet with the Cold War.

At one point, British troops were withdrawn from the Suez Canal area at the north end of the Red Sea. This left a big question mark concerning the future of that vital canal, so necessary in shipping.

On the home front, we three attended a First Communion party in the Gasthaus for Henny (Henrietta), one of the family's girls. There was lots of food and gaiety while Scott chewed and teethed on more Bavarian rolls. We were treated like part of the family and enjoyed it tremendously. This whole family and the maid, Helen, spoke English which was a big help. A youngish German woman also worked for them, usually hauling cases of beer up from the cellar. She spoke no English, but always greeted us cheerfully. She was not married, but obviously pregnant. Later, when she was in labor, Barbara had to drive her to the civilian hospital and later took family members to see her. The men of the family rode motorcycles, so the women had no means of travel. We were glad to help.

There was great excitement in the household over Barbara's father's retirement from the New York Telephone Company. A Hawaiian party was planned in Albany, since the Holmes were planning a trip to Hawaii. The party planners in Albany decided it would be a great idea to have them talk on the phone with us in the middle of the party. Our landlords were very excited with phone calls coming from the States to organize this, and they purchased a listening device for us. This meant that while one of us could talk, the other could listen in. We received details as to the day and time of the call, since we were 6 time zones apart. It went off very well, and the audience at the dinner party in Albany could hear the whole conversation through loudspeakers. That was the first Barbara had spoken with her parents and it was very heartwarming.

No one had warned us about spring spruce-up The Schreiders repainted rooms in the Gasthaus, but, without telling us, they also had the chimney sweep come and do his thing. Barb wondered why the furniture and the baby had a grayish tinge, and ended up scrubbing everything. Being at the bottom of the chimney didn't help. Another disadvantage turned up one day. One of our windows became clouded by a huge stack of cabbages. They were there for Opa (grandpa) to make sauerkraut by stomping on the cabbages barefoot in a huge tub.

Late in June, in Poznan, Poland, violence erupted as a result of anti-communist protests.

This was another unsettling event to add to the Cold War list.

Life in another country where you do not speak the language has its drawbacks. I found this to be true in the area of auto repairs. One day, our little Opel with its manual shift got stuck in first gear and wouldn't shift up. I needed to take it to the Autodienst (garage), but was self conscious about driving through the middle of Regensburg in first gear. I persuaded a friend in another Company to go with me. We laughed and laughed as I drove with one foot on the clutch and one on the gas pedal - ahead and coast, ahead and coast. But, the mechanics were nice and fixed the gearshift shaft right away, and back we went to Fort Skelly.

Barbara's Aunt Agnes Holme was on a tour of Europe and arranged to detour during the trip to spend time with us. She arrived by train and stayed at the Maximilian Hotel where we had been earlier. She was a good sport about our simple living conditions and enjoyed short sightseeing trips around the area. Having no experience with children, she still enjoyed seeing our son and heir, the first of our families to be able to do so.

At one point that month I had to go with the Battalion on maneuvers. Sgt. Edmonds outfitted the Supply truck with ice chests for some really good food, and it was warm enough to sleep under the stars. One night, as I lay sleeping under a very tall pine tree, I was awakened by a bird high over my head. I have always enjoyed hearing owls in the night when camping, but was astonished to hear a cuckoo. It was an extremely clear call, almost like a dream.

July was a pleasant month for us and warm. The Scheiders added furniture to the front terrace of the Gasthaus for a nice café area. Barbara and I often sat out there and read or played chess, with the basement window open so we could hear in case Scotty cried.

We took a one week vacation and drove south to a resort farther south in Bavaria on Lake Chiemsee. Our first sighting of the Bavarian Alps was dramatic, as we drove along the Autobahn (super highway) expectantly. The US Armed Forces had taken possession of three former Nazi resorts near the southern border of West Germany and made these available to the occupying forces. The one at Chiemsee was organized for families, with the right equipment, a playground, a beach, boats, and available baby sitters.

One day, we left Scotty with a sitter and took a boat ride to an island which held a large palace, a smaller replica of the Palace of Versailles in France. Mad King Ludwig II of Bavaria had no family but spent a lot of money building lavish palaces. This one was beautiful. In some rooms a coat of Dresden China covered the walls instead of wallpaper! Our guide told us with enthusiasm and gratitude that, in the final days of the War, General Eisenhower had issue orders that no GIs were to touch any of the artifacts in the Palace during its capture. Well done, Ike.

Another day, we three went up one of the Alps in a cable car, after Barbara and I decided we would all die together instead of leaving Scott on the ground. How sensible. As the car dangled from its cable, the landscape became more barren. We got off at the top, walked around a curve in the path, and there was a lovely Gasthaus, beer and all, of course. The view from there was breathtaking.

We returned to Regensburg well rested after an enjoyable time. However, we discovered that "we" were in the family way again. Scott was seven months old, and growing so fast that we had open mindedly decided to try for another child. We KNEW that it takes awhile to get pregnant, because, after all. it had the first time. WRONG! But we did not come unglued and were happy about it. This was some girl I married.

Within the last few days of the month, Egypt's ruler, Nasser, declared the nationalization of the Suez Canal. This was a very scary event that would lead to bigger problems in the future.

Another shocking event that month was the collision of two ocean liners off the island of Nantucket, Massachusetts, resulting in the sinking of one. The Stockholm, the Swedish ship Barbara had sailed to Germany, sliced its ice-cutting bow into the side of the Italian ship, Andrea Doria, causing it to sink after the Stockholm backed out. The world was shocked. Between the two ships there were many injured and 52 deaths. Other ships came to rescue survivors, and the Stockholm limped into New York . It was later determined that the Andrea Doria used improper radar procedures and made a wrong turn at the last minute. It all brought back reminders of the Titanic loss of 1912. Liners were still the major means of crossing the Atlantic at that time.

And so, the world braced for the next act of this dramatic era.

CHAPTER ELEVEN

The Tensions Increase

August was a very pleasant month for the 6th Armored Calvary with the usual rotations to border patrol. I never went on those trips, but stayed back to "mind the store," a perfect arrangement. At one point I went there with a jeep's trailer full of clean clothes to take to I Company troops and pick up dirty clothes to bring back to Quartermaster Laundry. Our communications guy did the driving, as I was not cleared to drive Army vehicles. Along the way we spied the remains of a small castle, parked the jeep and trailer behind bushes and toured. No guide, but there was a small brochure in a rack. Very interesting.

While delivering the clothes, we were sent right up to the border postings. There our Regiment had bunkers with 50 caliber machine guns pointed across the line at watch towers, where machine guns were pointed our way. Halfway between were a length of heavy concertino wire and rows of concrete tank traps. It was a warm Sunday, and, ironically, on the other side of the fence a couple strolled pushing a baby carriage. My companion and I, as well as the guys in the bunker, were completely at ease and enjoyed the view. What a world!

the fairly primitive machine really beat up the clothes. The cost for us was that Barbara's hands got more and more cracked and then the cracks collected coal dust from handling the stove. She didn't really complain, but I felt badly.

Barbara's parents planned a guided tour in Europe for later in the month and arranged to leave the tour for about four days with us. The Schreiders were excited and insisted that the Holmes stay in one of their bedrooms. We were excited, too, and figured out how to entertain them. Thank goodness we had moved to the better accommodations before they came.

However, before they came, the Hungarians rose up against their communist regime. Thus, October, 1956, became a pivotal month, in terms of the Cold War, with conflicts in several places. As mentioned in the Prologue, we wondered what might happen in Czechoslovakia. Might they decide to catch us off guard and invade West Germany? All leaves and time off were cancelled, and preparations began for the possible evacuation of dependents.

Because we had a car, Barbara would drive, carrying other dependents with her. She was given a list of instructions and a list of what we were to have ready for her to take. It was a little absurd - a number of bottles of baby formula ready at all times, for instance. They also issued her two decks of seven punched IBM cards each for her and Scott. These were to be used to pass through checkpoints on the way to LeHavre, France, to board a Navy ship. Regular US Army dog tags were issued for Scott, since he was not on a separate passport from Barbara's. One day, there was even a practice run, but it was just everyone meeting to see how it might go.

David and Goliath frieze in the old part of Regensburg

In spite of the tension, we had a good visit with the Holmes, and they were thrilled to meet their first grandchild. Because of my limited time off, we only visited places in Regensburg and nearby. There was plenty to see in Regensburg - old buildings, bridges and walls. We all enjoyed the time together, despite the overall worry of the Hungarian situation. Barbara's mother was also a little concerned about our having another baby so soon. They then went on their way to Switzerland to catch up with the tour.

Meanwhile, we were hearing stories about the numbers of people escaping from Hungary. Years later, James Michener wrote a small, non-fiction book about that. "The Bridge at Andau" refers to a spot on the northwest corner of Hungary where hundreds fled through marshland and over the bridge. Michener was a correspondent there at that time, and he listed the huge numbers of citizens of valuable professions who left. It is an incredible description of the problems of escaping and the eventual loss of interest of the guards in trying to stop anyone from fleeing - a very good read (see Appendix).

Then, in the last week of October, Israel invaded the Sinai Peninsula, and the Suez Crisis was under way. A few days later, Britain and France bombed the Egyptian airfields. As November began Gaza fell to the British and the Suez situation reached a cease fire. Then, the United Nations passed a resolution to send international troops.

November was fairly routine. In late autumn, the hoar-frost covered lawns and fields each morning, usually melting by 10:00 AM. On Election Day in the US, President Eisenhower was re-elected for another term. Also, the Army decided to change colors of its uniforms. Our first job, was for all soldiers to dye their boots and shoes black, so around the barracks that was under way. The brown uniforms would be dark blue, but not until after I left.

Barbara and I begin thinking of our coming trip home. By Thanksgiving I would be considered a "short-timer", someone whose tour of duty was due to end in less than a month. We were counting the days. I was even visited by someone from Battalion Headquarters trying to persuade me to re-enlist. No way!

Sure enough, before Thanksgiving my (actually "our") orders arrived for transportation by train on Dec. 9 to Bremerhaven. The document was followed a few days later by an amendment stating that we were to board the USS General Hodges*, sailing on Dec. 10.

Now, to get ready!

---

* This would be its last voyage as a troop ship. A year later it was used to bring Hungarian refugees to the United States.

CHAPTER TWELVE

Conflicts Or Not - We Are Going Home!

Our first concern was what to take home with us. Certainly not the car, but we did have baby equipment. After talking with the Quartermaster Office, I learned that we were entitled to ship 100 pounds of possessions for free and that, if we wanted, Quartermaster people would build a crate for another 100 pounds that we would pay to ship. A good plan, so I arranged for that. Barbara's steamer trunk would be about 100 pounds when packed, so baby items would go in a crate.

Timing was tricky. We wanted the car and the baby furniture right up to the last minute, and that did work out. I sold the car and the carpenters came and measured our collective baby gear. We took the carriage, the crib, high chair, playpen and changing table, and it all fit. We also packed the two suitcases Barbara had brought over, and my duffel bag.

There was still much to do. I had to turn in my field gear and personal weapon, which was already at the Company Armory (a pistol, Colt .45 I think). We said goodbye to various friends and fellow soldiers and bought up jars of baby food for the trip. We told our families not to try to meet us in Brooklyn, as we were not given an expected landing date. Oh, and we had Scott's 1st birthday on the 7th, two days before leaving. Barb didn't know it, but I also found time to buy three Hummel figurines for her for Christmas. We had shipped Christmas presents home ahead of time, including a Hummel for each of our mothers. They cost about 10 Deutsches Marks ($2.50) each then and are worth about $100 each now. I hid the three in my AWOL (Absent Without Leave) bag. This was like a small gym bag for socks, underwear, toiletries, Christmas cards to be addressed, and Hummel Figures. We also had a diaper bag and Barbara's cosmetics bag.

Our Christmas Card was a photo of Scotty in his Bavarian boy's clothes, even Lederhosen (leather shorts), sitting on a pile of suitcases ready to travel to the "Land Where Nickels Clink." You will read more about the cards later. You will wonder how I was going to get all of this plus a pregnant wife and a 30-pound child who didn't walk on and off trains etc. I wondered myself and indulged in prayer to a greater extent than usual. In some earlier tough spots I had asked for wisdom and strength, and God helped steady me, so it was even more needed now.

Around this time, we also paid attention to world news. The "Stars and Stripes" was great that way. There was more frightening news in the Cold War. The insurgence of Communism began in South Vietnam, supported by North Vietnam. This did not bode well for anything even slightly resembling world peace.

We took our money out of the American Express bank but didn't have to notify the Army Post Office (APO225), since a copy of my orders was sent there. We said a sad Farewell to our nice Gasthaus family, and Sgt. Fincher drove us to the Bahnhoff (rail station) where we had tickets already for a Second Class compartment, which we had all to ourselves. The trip to Aschaffenburg was quite pleasant, far better than what was to come. As we paused in the Nuremburg Bahnhoff on the way, I noticed that the whole roof was now completely reconstructed by the industrious Germans We pulled into the Aschaffenburg station in the early afternoon. Now the fun begins.

I had to physically get us and our bags (some heavy) onto the platform and then into the terminal. There were no porters or carts, so I did it in phases leaving Barbara and Scott at one end or the other of my trek and hoping the bags not attended wouldn't disappear. Miraculously, it worked.

Next, find some lunch. There were sandwiches available, but how to heat baby food. Except for rolls, Scott still ate Junior Food. I tried to explain to a restaurant about setting the jar in hot water (heis Waser), but wasn't understood. I even showed how to do it with my hands, which was not a problem for a Conroe. We fed him any way and added a roll.

Now I had to find the American train we were to board for the trip to Bremerhaven. I searched. I asked in halting German (Vo ist der Americanischer Zug?), but was told there wasn't one. I was getting really worried, not knowing what time it was scheduled to leave or what track it was on. Finally, I was going back to tell Barb and ran into two American MPs (Military Police) coming the other way. Now I could ask in English! Before I could open my mouth, one of the handsome young critters said," Are you Conroe?" I could have kissed him. They had been searching all over for us and were getting concerned, too. As an added bonus, here were two more sets of muscles to help carry everything. We hurried to Barbara, and the transfer was accomplished quickly. Talk about help appearing when most needed! I heaved a huge sigh of relief and fatigue as we boarded the train. It left the station shortly after we arrived.

We were given our own compartment with triple stacked bunks on one wall and told when dinner and breakfast would be served.

I assumed the MPs had reported us "Present and accounted for." Whew! After a nice supper and warmed Gerbers jars, we tried to figure out where each of us would sleep. The pregnant lady and the chubby one year old should be near the floor, so they crammed into the bottom bunk, and I took the next bunk up. We didn't sleep well, but at least we were on our way and on the right track. Pun intended.

The next morning, we enjoyed good coffee and a nice breakfast. Looking out the window, everything was gray and dismal. What can you expect on the North Sea in December? The train pulled into Bremerhaven and stopped directly next to the pier. There sat our ship, the Hodges, with American flags flying in the breeze, looking just as gray as the landscape. I must say, it was a luxury to have sailors from the ship handle our pile of luggage so I could carry Scott.

I had been told before-hand that only Sergeants and above had cabins with their wives, and we other accompanied soldiers would be in a large triangular bunkroom in the bow of the ship, while our wives and children would be in cabins with other wives. There were only two of us in our condition. That is, pregnant wives with a one year old child each who needed to be carried and fed. We approached the Navy officers together, but it was no go. We even promised not to touch the better food in the officers and dependants dining room, if we could help our wives. But no, no exceptions could be made against military rules. Luckily, Barbara had three very nice young wives in her cabin who helped her and, later, even baby sat while we met for a movie.

The USS General Hodges in dock at Bremerhaven, W. Germany

The icing on the cake was the setup of rules governing when I could see my family. For the first half of the voyage, it would be from 2-4 in the afternoon, and, from the middle of the trip, it would be 7-9 in the evening. Wasn't that grand of the Navy?

Well, we'll have to figure out something better on our own, I said to the New Jersey architect in the same fix.

And we did. In fact, you will discover as you read about the rest of the tale of the homeward bound, we actually got away with a few things by being inventive, and we didn't touch the food in the officers and dependents dining room, and I never told the Army or the Navy.

CHAPTER THIRTEEN

The Long Voyage: This Isn't Kansas, Toto!

Now we settled into our shipboard locations--me with a lot of other husbands one deck down from the open deck and Barbara on the next lower deck in a large cabin with four bunks and a crib in the middle of the floor. Some white hats (Navy term for sailors) carried her bags down there, while I dragged my duffel bag to the husbands' quarters. As soon as I got there, I checked my AWOL bag to make sure the Hummel figures were still OK. Then the ship sailed, complete with a band playing while the gangplank was removed. That was December 10.

I was given a daily assignment, as I had on the way over. My job was to "police" the open deck, that is, pick up papers and debris. But, for the whole voyage, the deck was off limits due to waves of sea water often washing over it. Therefore, I had nothing to do and assigned myself the task of addressing Christmas cards to be mailed whenever we got to the US. Of course, being in the most forward compartment in the bow, we went up and down like an elevator all day and all night. The north Atlantic in December is not a great place to be. If Scott had required a special formula, we would have been flown home, but there we were. It was supposed to be a nine day trip, but we altered our course to get away from a storm. The storm followed us, and the trip ended up being thirteen days. Luckily, it was not iceberg season, which I just read starts in January when the sun starts warming the ice.

Barbara and I would meet daily from 2-4 in the main lounge, which was well decorated for Christmas. I got a kick out of watching youngsters about 5 years old standing in the middle of the floor like there was no floor movement. They simply leaned one way and then the other and so on. Barb could take Scotty to a playroom on the next lower deck in the mornings. The New Jersey architect and I learned how to sneak around the ladder well guard and get in there to see our families some more.

Barbara and I would compare notes as to how we were surviving the voyage. She had a problem with the Navy's insisting on a daily mid-morning inspection when Scott was napping. She finally burst into tears one morning, and they decided they could ignore that cabin. Late in the trip, the motion bothered her stomach, so she began carrying a barf bag. They were readily available, several stuck in the passage hand rails. Scott thought she was playing peek-a-boo.

A little help with the monotony was a daily bulletin of comics, information about the voyage and schedules. The last full day at sea (Dec. 21), there was a special souvenir edition which I have kept ever since. In it was a poem dedicated to the poor guys in a troop ship following behind us who might not make it home for Christmas. The Navy had scheduled our ship to dock ahead of the other one, so they would have to wait for us before they could enter the Brooklyn Navy Yard.

We finally pulled into dock on Saturday, December 22. I had arranged for a room for us at Fort Hamilton, the Army base where I would be processed. However, we looked up at the crowd overlooking the dock, and there was Barbara's brother, Gordon! After commenting that Barbara hadn't changed at all, even the same maternity dress as when she had left, he happily took his sister and nephew off to the Albany area. He lived in New Jersey and was going to his parents for Christmas.

It took all day Sunday to be processed out. I had turned in my reserved room, but another husband, whose wife had been met earlier, and I found we could get into my room through a connecting door. So, we put the mattress on the floor for me, and he slept on the box spring. In the middle of the night, the door opened, and the light went on. The concierge was showing an officer and his wife where they could stay. We didn't move a muscle, and they disappeared in confusion.

We were finally released, not discharged, in the late afternoon, including distribution of money for unused leave and a $300 mustering out payment from the State of New York. We were allowed to keep our uniforms and duffel bag, but had to relinquish either the overcoat or the field jacket. I kept the overcoat. Then we were given our release orders. Hooray! The Army gave us dinner, and then a group of us got a taxi to take us to Grand Central Station in Manhattan for trains home. Mine got into Albany at about 1:00 AM. I took a cab to Delmar, found the key that my in-laws kept in the garage, let myself in, and fell asleep in my father-in-law's armchair.

The next day, I was discovered asleep. After a nice day of verbal catching up, we went to my parents' house in Altamont for Christmas Eve dinner. They and my brother and sister would finally meet the newest family member from West Germany. It was wonderful and very fitting, since this was the house where I had received the Draft notice two years earlier. My father even modeled the Lederhosen we had sent him, and both fathers had new Bavarian pipes. We were quite proud of ourselves for pulling off the awful trip.

71

After dinner, there were presents. That included the ones we had shipped ahead and a whole coffee table piled high with packages for us. We were overwhelmed, to be sure.

Now, on to the new year and putting our civilian life back together, including getting that new Norge washer out of storage. Now, Barbara would not have to suffer coal dust in the cracks in her hands, from washing by hand, any more or ever again.

As an add-on to this chapter, I should also mention that we never did have to pay for the 100 pounds of goods the Army shipped. In the confusion, Barb's big trunk went on one ship with a copy of my orders, and the crate the Army built went on a different ship with a copy of my orders. Each was thought to be *the* free 100 pounds, and we never told them anything different.

CHAPTER FOURTEEN

The Last Of The 1950s

Early in January of 1957, the United States committed itself to the Eisenhower doctrine. What this meant was that we would aid in defending Iran, Pakistan and Afghanistan from the danger of communism.

Everything seemed to fall into place for our little family in 1957. I resumed teaching math in North Syracuse, New York, in a newly built high school building. I rented a room and looked for a rental house, finding a small ranch that was perfect. We retrieved our furniture and other possessions, looking forward to the birth of our next child.

In February, I received word from the US Army that I was now assigned to a Ready Reserve unit. It was a tank battalion in Long Island City, New York. I did not have to report there unless there was a national calamity.

David Craig Conroe arrived at 1:30 AM on April 5th, after a tense drive in very wet snow to St. Mary's Maternity Hospital on the north side of Syracuse. The evening before, Barbara was restless and felt the beginnings of contractions. I was relieved when she said "Let's go" (this became our routine in future births), and I bundled Scotty into his snowsuit for the ride. I couldn't stay at the hospital because of Scott which Barbara already knew. So, we came home, and he went back to bed while I corrected math papers and waited anxiously for the phone call from our doctor, telling me we had another son and all was well with mother and baby.

After a sleepless night, I fed and dressed Scott and took him with me to school after phoning in that a substitute teacher would be needed. I took homeroom attendance with Scott holding court in the middle of my desk. The 8th graders were thrilled.

Summer was very nice, and the Cold War held no major events. Barbara and I decided to look into the housing market to see what we could buy. Our rented house was for sale, but we thought we could find something a little nicer. We did. We found a nice six-room Cape Cod style house for sale by its owners. After a few discussions and small loan from Barb's parents, it was ours. The owners had us over to meet the neighbors one evening, and we seemed to pass muster. We moved in before the school year started.

By October, the world knew of the nuclear capability of the USSR, so our Strategic Air Command initiated a 24/7 nuclear alert. It stayed in place until 1991, in case of a Soviet surprise attack occurred by way of their ICBM (InterContinental Ballistic Missiles).

Soon after that, the USSR launched its first spatial satellite, Sputnik. The space race was on. By November, Sputnik 2 was launched, bearing a live being, a dog named Laika, into space.

In November, a special committee appointed by President Eisenhower determined that our country was far behind the USSR in missile capabilities. The committee also recommended that the US establish a vigorous movement to build fallout shelters. In schools, we began to look at a new form of the familiar fire drill called "duck and cover." This involved students diving under their desks or going to a shelter area in the basement. It reminded me of air raid drills during

World War II, wherein students would rush home, usually taking with us other students who lived in surrounding villages.

In 1958, there were six important events for the world to consider. First, in Iraq, there was a major revolution wherein the pro-British Shah was removed and forced into exile. Then, Iraq began close ties with the Soviet Union which would continue through the Cold War.

In August, 1958 two events added to world tension. China began bombing Quemoy, which created the second Taiwan Strait Crisis. That same month, the US deployed Intermediate Range Ballistic Missiles (IRBMs) to England, which put them in range of Moscow.

Then in September, a US reconnaissance plane was shot down by Russian MIGs over Armenia. There were 17 casualties.

October, 1958 was when the United States formed NASA, the National Aeronautics and Space Administration. We were becoming more serious about space exploration.

This month I received another US Army letter with a questionnaire that I could submit. The purpose was to explain why I should be transferred to a Standby Reserve unit, only called up in a major war. This would be based on having a vital occupation. I sent it explaining my status as a high school mathematics teacher. Earlier I mentioned that I would not have been drafted in 1955 if they had known I was teaching math then.

November brought another Berlin crisis when Nikita Khrushchev asked the western nations to withdraw from that city. They did not.

November 10 I received a new assignment to the Standby Reserve unit in Camp Kilmer, New Jersey. I was very pleased to note in that set of orders that I had been promoted to Specialist 4, which was equivalent to Sergeant.

A really positive highlight of the year for the US occurred in Moscow. Twenty-three year-old Van Cliburn of Texas won the first quadrennial Tchaikovsky Piano Competition, which had to be embarrassing for the Soviets, but good for morale here.

1959 began with the advent of the Cuban Revolution. Fidel Castro became Cuba's leader, but avoided any statement that the country had become communist. From that activity, guerilla activities sprang up across Latin America.

In July, Vice President Nixon visited Moscow for the opening of the American National Exhibition. While there, he and Khrushchev debated the military capacities of each other.

August ushered in a progressive step in the space adventures for the US. We launched Explorer 6 into orbit with equipment for photographing the earth from space.

In December, the FNL (Viet Cong) was formed in North Vietnam as a Communist movement vowing to remove the anti-communist dictatorship in South Vietnam. This was not a good note upon which to end the decade.

CHAPTER FIFTEEN

Will The 1960s Be Better Internationally?

Looking at the list of events in this decade, it seems to be the most calamitous ten years of the Cold War, both for the world generally and for the United States specifically. There were coups and revolutions in various parts of the world, increasing nuclear tensions between the major powers, a major war in southeast Asia, and three horrendous assassinations in the US.

In early 1960, France entered the nuclear scene when it tested its first atomic bomb in the Algerian Sahara Desert.

Also early in the year, Barbara became pregnant with our third child, after having the experience of a miscarriage in the fall before. We were hoping for a girl, of course.

In April, the US deployed IRBMs to Italy, in addition to those in Britain and even closer to Moscow.

A major shock came when the Soviets shot down a US U-2 spy plane over their territory. The pilot, Francis Gary Powers, survived and was taken prisoner. This became known as the U-2 Incident in conversations and headlines everywhere, embarrassing the US. In June, the Chinese split from connection to the USSR, who treated them as second class citizens. Now there were three dimensions to the Cold War.

In Laos, in August, the communist Pathet Lao started a revolution.

October was the month for our next birthing experience. Barbara's parents were on standby to come and help us, but after the birth. We arranged with our next door neighbors for help in an emergency. If needed in the middle of a night, Connie would come over and get in our bed while we two went to St. Mary's. At about 3:00 AM on October 12th, Barbara had contractions, so I called next door. We were lucky in the timing, as Connie and her husband were leaving town on the 12th for an architects' convention. Whew! On the way to the hospital, Barbara said that, if this was another boy, I should have a urinal installed before she got home. It wasn't needed. Laurie Jean was born at 6:30 and I got back home at about 7:30. Our neighbor asked what I was doing THERE. I told her proudly of our daughter's birth, which she thought wasn't fair. She had had 30 hours of labor with each of two children. The day being Columbus Day, I didn't have to go to school, and, because it was a Wednesday that year, I had a five-day weekend, and the Holmes, Barbara's parents, came on the weekend to stay a week.

The year 1961 held several events of worldwide interest:

January:

President Eisenhower closed the US embassy in Havana and severed relations with Cuba

John F. Kennedy was inaugurated as US President.

February:

An insurgency began in Angola against Portuguese rule.

April:

On the 12th (my birthday), Uri Gagarin was the first human in space and first to orbit the earth after the Soviet Union had launched Vostok I.

On the 17th, Cuba was invaded at the Bay of Pigs by a counter-military force of Cuban exiles supported and trained by our CIA. They attacked coming from Guatemala and hoped to overthrow Fidel Castro's leftist government, but they were defeated two days later. It was an embarrassment for the United States.

May:

President Kennedy announced the intent of the United States to put a man on the moon, initiating the Apollo program.

June:

The US deployed IRBMs to Turkey, again positioning those weapons closer to Moscow. Britain and Italy were still bases for potential launches, too.

August:

The Berlin Wall was built after the breakdown of talks concerning the continued occupation of that city. Thus began decades of separation of Germans east to west and the determination of many people to escape to West Germany.

October:

In Berlin, Checkpoint Charlie became the focal point of a standoff between Soviet and US tanks.

The Soviet Union detonated the Tsar Bomba, the most powerful thermonuclear weapon ever tested.

In 1962, there were fewer tension-filled events, but one of those was considerably more serious. In February, American AU-2 pilot, Francis Gary Powers was exchanged for a senior KGB spy, Colonel Rudolf Abel.

Some good things happened for the Conroe family. I had been studying at Syracuse University under the GI Bill, thinking I would want to move up to being a Principal someday. However, the high school where I worked had an opening for someone to be a halftime Guidance Counselor and halftime teacher for a year, to be followed by full time Counselor. I would have to be certified and have two years of successful teaching experience. I had all but one required course for certification, so took that in the summer. This job would be 11 months a year instead of 10, so I would no longer have to look for summer employment.

Barbara and I also decided that our cute Cape was getting too small for the five of us. That summer we found a new colonial with 4 bedrooms and 2 ½ baths. Wow! The price was right, so we moved about 5 blocks, although we hated to leave our neighbors.

In September, Chinese forces attacked India, starting the Himalayan War, which ended in November. At the end China occupied a strip of Indian Territory.

October brought the very scary Cuban Missile Crisis. The Soviets had secretly delivered nuclear weapons to Cuba, and President Kennedy ordered a blockade of the island when that was discovered. This brought the two nations to the brink of war, but after negotiations, the Soviets backed down and removed the missiles, with an agreement by the US to remove our missiles from Turkey. We also promised to not move against Cuba.

January 1963 brought another document from the United States Army. It was a set of orders and a certificate for my final (and Honorable) discharge from service as of December 31, 1962. It also stated that I received the Good Conduct Medal.

During the first half of 1963, the Cold War was fairly calm. In June, the United States set up a hotline with the Soviets to make communication better. In the same month, France announced the withdrawal of its navy from the North Atlantic fleet of NATO.

In July, the Partial Test Ban Treaty was signed by the UK, the US and the USSR. This prohibited any testing of nuclear weapons above ground.

November 1963 brought disaster. First, the Prime Minister of South Vietnam was assassinated in a coup, which was suspected to have been aided by our CIA.

On the 22nd of November, US President John F. Kennedy was shot and killed in Dallas, Texas, while on a campaigning tour with Mrs. Kennedy. Lee Harvey Oswald was the sniper and was shot and killed while being transported between prisons. That shooter, Jack Ruby, died in prison of a heart attack several days later. Lyndon B. Johnson, the Vice President, was sworn into office aboard Air Force One, as it was being readied to fly to Washington with the Johnsons, Mrs. Kennedy and President Kennedy's remains. The country and the world were shocked.

Nineteen sixty four began with the decision of Barbara and me that this would be a good time to have a fourth (and last) child. Our offspring were now 8, 6 and 3, and we had talked early in our marriage about having four children. Conception was successful with a due date in late October.

At some point in this time frame, the Soviet Politburo voted to increase its funding for terrorism by 1,000%. How is that for putting the world on notice?

On the positive side of things, this was also the year of the Beatles' first appearance on television's Ed Sullivan Show. They arrived in the US on February 7. American teenagers, as well as some older than that, went crazy over their performances.

In March, a military coup in Brazil overthrew the elected president, whose proposals for improving the nation looked communistic to our military.

In April, President Johnson and Soviet Premier Khrushchev simultaneously announced plans to reduce production of materials needed in making nuclear weapons.

On August 4th, President Johnson claimed that North Vietnamese naval vessels had fired on two American destroyers in the Gulf of Tonkin. It was claimed that the American ships were in North Vietnam waters, but that was later proved unfounded. This incident led to the open involvement of the US in the Vietnam War.

In October, 1964, Leonid Brezhnev succeeded Khrushchev as General Secretary of the Communist Party of the USSR. That same month, China tested its first atomic bomb, bringing the total of the world's nuclear powers to five.

On October 21st, right on schedule, John Davis Conroe joined our family. That was the actual due date. Our other three were each born before their due date, but they got closer with each one. Barbara's mother had warned us that she could no longer handle this many kids, so my mother, said she would come. And she came ahead of the birth! She had one day to see how the older three were fed and prepared for school or pre-school, and John came at 6:30 the next morning. This time, the St. Mary's nuns treated me to coffee and Danish while I awaited word from upstairs.

Mother stayed a week, and then we hired a wonderful lady who came in each weekday for three weeks. She fed the kids their breakfast and got them on their way to the day's activities. We also treated ourselves to diaper service, that being still the days of cloth diapers that had to be laundered. Life was good.

Chapter Sixteen

The Last Half Of The 1960s

In March of 1965, the United States began a military build up to help defend South Vietnam. North Vietnam also committed troops to the war. The US also began sustained bombing of North Vietnam.

In April, the US military invaded the Dominican Republic, which shares the island of Hispaniola in the Caribbean Ocean with Haiti. The object was prevention of another communist presence like in Cuba.

Later in the spring, I learned that a colleague at Solvay High School, on the western edge of Syracuse, was retiring as Director of Guidance. This seemed like an opportunity for more responsibility and salary, so I applied and was offered the job. It was a smaller school with only one other counselor, a former teacher I had known at North Syracuse. She worked with the 9th and 10th graders, while I had the Juniors and Seniors. It meant a one-half hour commute with our only car, but I often hurried home so Barbara could take the car for shopping.

During the summer I received a phone call from an earlier fellow graduate student at Alfred. He was now in Syracuse working at Onondaga Community College as Director of Continuing Education. He asked if I would be willing to teach math there at night. It would be two classes on two nights. I always enjoyed teaching and agreed. Now I had income from my fulltime job, teaching at night, and the

GI Bill. I was still working on a High School Principal certificate. This worked well for our needs without requiring Barbara to work. She really enjoyed the role of housewife.

That August, a second Indian-Pakistani War broke out on the 15th of the month.

September 23rd marked the end of that war through a cease-fire. At the end of that month six Indonesian generals were murdered as part of a coup called the 30 September Movement.

On November 14th, the Battle of Ia Drang occurred in Vietnam. It was the first battle between US troops and regular Vietnamese forces.

As the war continued in Vietnam, only three other dangerous events occurred in nineteen sixty-six. In March, France withdrew from the NATO command structure, in May, Communist China detonated its third atomic bomb, and the South African Border War began in August. Three different continents were thus involved,

Again, in 1967, world tensions popped up on various continents. In March, General Suharto was successful in overthrowing Sukarno as President of Indonesia.

In April, Latin American and Caribbean nations signed the Treaty of Tlatelolco in Mexico City. This treaty sought the prohibition of nuclear weapons in those two international areas of the Western Hemisphere.

Two major events occurred in May, 1967. Egypt blocked the Straits of Tiran, expelled the UN peacekeepers and placed its army in the Sinai Peninsula in case of an Israeli attack there. Then an uprising happened in Naxalbari, India, to mark the expansion of Maoism as a violent, anti-US and anti-Soviet insurgency across several third world countries.

On the personal side, I decided that, though I enjoyed my job, helping Seniors decide on colleges led me to think that a college town might be a good place to raise four children.

North Syracuse was a sprawling suburb with a huge school district. Next year, Scott would have to board a bus fairly early in the morning to go to middle school, another factor. By now, I had concluded my certification graduate work. With Barbara's agreement, I sent out resumes to colleges around the state and heard promptly from the Counseling Director at the State University College at Potsdam, way north almost to Canada. I was interviewed on tape at Howard Johnson's Motel by their traveling Personnel Director and later invited up north for a full interview. That went well and I was offered the job of Counselor starting in September.

In June, Israel did invade the Sinai Peninsula, as Egypt thought it might. This began the Six-Day War on the 23rd of the month.

In July, Barbara and I made trips to Potsdam to look at houses. There was not a big selection. One house had a garish color combination, so we were not interested, but I went back with a friend who had lots of older home experience. David went with us. My friend thought that the tall Victorian with 5 bedrooms could look better with different colors, so we went in. After discussion on the way home, I called the owner, made an offer, and was accepted. I should add that the kids' ages at this point were Scott 11 ½, David 10, Laurie 6 ½, and John 2 ½.

Early in August, the Bangkok Declaration was established to halt the spread of communist in Southeast Asia.

Later that month, we moved north, leaving our house with a serious sale offer. The new house allowed each of the children to have their own bedroom after David said he wanted the little former sewing room for his private space. It was a 2 ½ stories high Victorian built in the 1890s. Lots of space indoors and out, plus a barn. The location was great in that we could all walk to everything - schools, movies, Scouts, Public Library and houses of new friends. After settling in, it seemed to us that this had been an excellent move.

January 1968 was difficult internationally. On the 22nd, North Korea captured a US Navy electronic surveillance ship. The Captain of the USS Pueblo assumed he was in international waters when two fishing trawlers spotted the ship and reported it back to Pyongyang, the capital. A North Korean warship challenged the Navy ship to identify itself. This was the day after North Korean operatives had secretly crossed into South Korea, intent on murdering President Pak. All but one of them were killed. If the Pueblo's personnel had known of this, they might not have stayed so close to shore.

The Pueblo was not prepared for battle, with ice coating its guns, and after a short chase it was threatened by a torpedo fired from a North Korean ship. After being boarded and hand to hand fighting took place, the ship was captured (also after many records and some equipment were destroyed for security reasons), and the 83 American crew members, one of whom was wounded, were marched off the boat for confinement.

Later in January 1969, the Tet Offensive began in South Vietnam. Then in March, President Johnson suspended the US bombings of North Vietnam and announced that he would not seek re-election.

With our youngest son, John, now in Kindergarten, Barbara thought about what she might do for work. She began by taking Education courses to prepare for being an elementary reading teacher. My job was going well. I liked the variety of counseling students about academics, majors, future careers, and personal problems.

In June, the Tet Offensive ended in an American victory. However, it caused many anti-war protests on college campuses and led to conjecture about our military chances in Vietnam.

We added a puppy to our household - a black retriever mix. Stacey (Anastasia of St. Lawrence) was a great addition. Rascal the cat ignored her.

In Communist Czechoslovakia, in August, the Prague Spring Reforms resulted in Warsaw Pact intervention, which crushed them.

December ended the year on a bitter note. The captain and crew of the USS Pueblo were released by North Korea, after a year of poor diet, lies, beatings and torture. The ship is still in North Korea, where it is a tourist attraction, but it is still considered by the US Navy to be a commissioned ship.*

On January 20, 1969, Richard Nixon was sworn in as the new US President.

In March, there were border clashes between the Soviet Union and China. Then, later, the United States began bombing Communist hideouts in Cambodia.

On July 20, the US accomplished the first ever manned moon landing; the space ship was Apollo 11, which carried the Lunar Exploration Module (LEM). The latter carried Neil Armstrong and Buzz Aldrin from the ship to the moon's surface. This was a hugely acclaimed feat, bringing pride to our country.

Later in July, the United States began withdrawing its troops from Vietnam. This left the South Vietnamese military to handle the REMAINING combat there.

On September 1, Muammar al-Gaddafi overthrew the monarchy of Libya and expelled British and American personnel. The new government made it clear that it was a close ally of the Soviet Union, bringing more worries to the world scene

---

* Information gathered from the website "damninteresting.com/the seizing-of-the-Pueblo".

Chapter Seventeen

Now A Look At The 1970s

1970 - In March the Nuclear Non-Proliferation Treaty was signed by the US, the United Kingdom, the Soviet Union and others. On the 18th, Lon Nol took power in Cambodia. The Khmer Rouge and Vietnamese Communists attacked the new government, which had wanted to remove the Vietnamese presence in Cambodia.

Although Barbara enjoyed the Education courses she took, she decided not to go ahead with the practice teaching required to become certified. With college educations starting with Scott in three years and John in school now all day, it seemed a good idea for Barbara to seek employment. Books and reading had always been one of her strong points, and the secretarial position opened in the Potsdam Public Library. She was offered the job, which included some front desk duty, and she jumped right in.

In November, the United States began sending aid to support the Lon Nol regime in Cambodia.

1971 - In February, South Vietnamese forces entered Laos in an attemmpt to cut the Ho Chi Minh trail.

Earlier, I had begun thinking about more graduate school for me to earn a doctorate. I really liked college work and realized that to be more professionally accepted I would need a Ph.D or an Ed.D.

After applications, I was accepted at State University at Albany for an Ed.D in counseling and student affairs management. With credit transferred in from Syracuse, I could do the doctorate with two summers, some independent study, one year of residency in Albany and, of course, the dissertation.

March 25th marked the third Indo-Pakistani War, and Bangladesh gained independence from Pakistan.

In late June, as I prepared to leave for six weeks of summer school in Albany, where I would be living with my parents except on weekends, I was summoned to the office of the Vice President for Academic Affairs at Potsdam. Surprisingly, he asked me if I would be interested in becoming the Assistant Vice President for Academic Affairs. I hadn't known that the man in that position was changing to being the head of Personnel (now called Human Resources).

I talked about this with the Acting President/Vice President for Student Affairs and with the man I would be replacing, as well as the head of Personnel. Over my four years in the Counseling Office, I had often sent students to him for final approval of credits, especially for transfer students. Now I would be able to do that, as well as manage the course schedule, registration of students, the academic calendar and whatever else the Vice President or the Acting President wanted me to do. I would also be an active member of the President's Cabinet.

I accepted, to begin September 1st, and went off to summer school. We now became a two car family, since I couldn't leave Barbara with four kids and a job to manage and no car.

On September 3rd, the United Kingdom, the Soviet Union, France, and the United States signed the Four-Power Agreement on Berlin.

On October 25th, the United Nations General Assembly passed a resolution recognizing the People's Republic of China as the only legitimate government of China.

On December 16, Bangladesh and Indian forces defeated Pakistan in the Bangladesh Liberation War. Bangladesh received the recognition of the eastern bloc of nations.

1972 - On February 21st, President Richard Nixon visited China. This was the first visit by a US President since the People's Republic was established. It was a major step in diplomacy and astonished the world.

May 26th marked the signing of the Strategic Arms Limitation Talks (SALT I) document. This marked the beginning of détente between the US and the USSR.

Another session of summer school at UAlbany for me. We were very fortunate that the college President set so much importance on faculty finishing doctor's degrees. We had a deal that if I invested my four weeks of annual vacation in graduate work, I could have the other two weeks with pay also.

On September, American chess player Bobby Fischer defeated Russian Boris Spassky in a match at Reykjavik, Iceland. He thus became the first official American chess champion on the world scene.

On December 18th, President Nixon announced that the US would begin massive bombings of North Vietnam.

1973 - January 27 marked the end of US involvement in the Vietnam War with the signing of the Paris Peace Accords. Congress stopped the funding for continued bombing of Indochina.

In June, Scott graduated from high school, starting our thirteen years of college funding. We were determined that all four kids would not incur loans. He would be off to St. Lawrence University in the Fall. He planned to major in English.

We would both be in higher education pursuits, as this academic year would find me in Albany. I turned over most of my job to a "stand in" faculty member and went to Albany Monday to Friday each week, while Barbara coped with three kids and her part time job.

Each weekend at home I spent Saturday in the office and overall managed to invest my vacation, also work holidays, and keep my salary coming.

In September a Chilean military coup occurred in which the elected president, Salvador Allende was deposed and committed suicide during the fighting.

At this time I presented my plan for the dissertation to a large panel of SUNY Albany's School of Education faculty. It was accepted. Now to get ready for the two-day doctoral qualifying exam.

October 6 was the day of the Yom Kippur War in which Israel was attacked by Egypt and Syria. The war ended in a ceasefire.

In November, the Soviet Union announced that it would not play in a World Cup soccer game against Chile if it were held in Santiago. Their reason was their opposition to the recent overthrow of President Allende in Chile.

Great news! I passed the important exam and finished the semester.

1974 - This was a fairly quiet year for the Cold War. It was the year of the Watergate Scandal in August, named for the break ins at that building in Washington in connection with Presidential campaigning. President Nixon was forced to resign, the first US president to do so, and Vice President Gerald Ford became President.

I finished my course work at Albany in the spring and went back to my job full time.

In my absence, the Academic Vice President had been forced to leave the position and return to teaching Physics. Therefore, I had to manage alone for the fall semester.

Scott was 18 and had to register for the Draft. Ugh!

In September, the pro-Western monarch of Ethiopia, Haile Selassie was ousted by a Marxist military group called the Derg.

During this academic semester, I collected data at both SUNY Potsdam and SUNY Plattsburgh relative to the needs of transfer students. My goal was to determine if transfers had more or less problems at college than did students who had been at their college starting as freshmen. I labeled them "natives".

I analyzed the data, which showed statistically significant results, but not as I had hypothesized. Over a list of eleven areas where students might have problems, students "native" to the college indicated more problems than did transfer students. This was the opposite of what other literature had described. It was true in both colleges, adding still more credence to the results. (A few years after I would publish an article about this in a national journal.)

Then I began writing the dissertation. I turned Scott's bedroom into my dissertation den and went there every night at 7:00, determined to finish this project. I had heard of others who had never received the degree because of not finishing the dissertation. That was not going to happen to me.

1975 - In January, My doctoral advisor went on sabbatical leave, so another faculty member stepped in. He took the approach that we would move ahead with the dissertation at a leisurely pace. When I said I was determined to finish the degree in May, he agreed.

Job-wise, I was asked by the President to become Assistant to the President and Coordinator of Academic Services. The Dean of Graduate Studies became Acting Vice President of Academic Affairs at the same time. I moved into the President's office complex and was responsible for the College Library, the Registrar, the Director of Sponsored Research, the Director of International Studies and the

Director of Media Arts and Technology, all of whom had been under the Vice President.

In April, two events in the Cold War occurred. The communist Khmer Rouge took over in Cambodia, followed by major genocide there, Known as "The Killing Fields". Also, North Vietnam defeated South Vietnam. It ended with the fall of Saigon, and the two countries became one under a communist government.

May brought more action in that area of the world. The Khmer Rouge seized an American naval ship. The US intervened to recapture the ship, and the crew was released.

That was also the month, after meetings of my doctoral committee and a few revisions in the dissertation, that I completed it and graduated, with all of my family there. What a day that was!

In June, Portugal withdrew from Angola and Mozambique, whereupon Marxist governments were installed in both. The civil war there involved Angolans, Mozambicans, South Africans and Cubans.

My family experienced another high school graduation. We proudly watched David walk across the stage. He would be going to Southampton College on Long Island in the fall to major in Marine Biology. He, too, had to register for the Draft.

The first joint flight of the US and Soviet Space programs happened successfully in July. It was labeled the Apollo-Soyuz Test Project.

1976 - There was not much world conflict that year. It should be noted that both the current Chinese Premier Zhou Enlai and Mao Zedong, who was responsible for so much communist suppression before him, died in January and September respectively, that year.

In March, a coup d'etat occurred in Argentina, causing a civil war there.

In July, the United States pulled its military personnel out of Thailand.

1977- That year, the Cold War was even quieter.

In January, Jimmy Carter became President of the United States.

In June, Scott Conroe graduated from St. Lawrence University and began seeking employment. He stayed at home sending out resumes and eventually got a job as editor of a weekly newspaper in a suburb of Syracuse.

In July, the Ogaden War began in Africa, when Somalia attacked Ethiopia.

1978 - On March 5, the Ogaden War ended with a cease-fire.

In April the President of Afghanistan's government was overthrown. He was murdered by pro-communist rebels.

At the end of the academic year, the Potsdam College President, who was my good friend and mentor, retired. His replacement and a new Vice President for Academic Affairs both arrived that summer.

June brought the Conroe family to its next high school graduation. Laurie "trod the boards" this time and was very excited about attending the SUNY College at Plattsburgh in the fall to study to become a nurse.

Early in the fall, the College President asked me to go with him to lunch downtown. Unusual, but I was curious. He asked me if I would be willing to move back over to Academic Affairs to help the new Vice President. He would replace me in his office with someone who would spend more time on computer based projects, and I would still have those reporting to me still with me. After some discussion, I agreed, but did not want to go back to the same title I had had. In academe, titles are important for some reason, so, similar to the levels of professorship, I became Associate Vice President. I still had his ear whenever I would need it.

A sad note for our family came with the death of Barbara's father, Furman Holme, on December 17. He was 82.

On December 25, a communist government was established in Afghanistan.

1979 - In January the Vietnamese deposed the Khmar Rouge and installed a pro-Soviet government. West of that area, Iran ousted the Shah and installed a theocracy.

In February, a Sino-Vietnamese War developed when China attacked North Vietnam because it had invaded Cambodia.

In May, war broke out in El Salvador between Communist insurgents and the US backed government.

May also brought a bright note in the graduation of David from Southampton College. He had added a Business Administration minor, but was still a Marine Biology major. He took two "years out west" for experience returning back east each summer to work in Southampton at the posh Meadow Club tennis club.

On June 18, President Carter and the Soviet Leader, Leonid Brezhnev signed the SALT II agreement, updating the list of limitations and guidelines for nuclear weapons.

In July of 1979, President Carter signed in the first wave of financial aid to opponents of the pro-Soviet regime in Afghanistan.

In September, the Marxist president of Afghanistan was deposed and murdered. His post was taken by Prime Minister Hafizullah Amin.

November 4th marked a terrible situation in Iran. Islamist students took over the American embassy and took all of the occupants hostage. This crisis lasted until January 20th, 1981, the day Ronald Reagan was sworn in as our new President.

On December 24th, the Soviet Union invaded Afghanistan to oust Amin, which led to the end of Détente.

CHAPTER EIGHTEEN

The 1980S Decade

The Cold War will Finally End Someday

For several reasons, I am now going to speed up the listing of the events in the 1980s. Every year brought major happenings, some good and some bad, and it seems, then, like it was time to bring this War to a close. You, dear reader, have been very patient in hanging with my writings right to the end, so let's pick up the momentum of the listings.

1980

February - The US Olympic Hockey Team defeated the Soviet Union in semi finals to go to the gold medal round against Finland, which it also won, in Lake Placid, N.Y.

March - The US and its allies boycotted the summer Olympics in Moscow

May -Josip Broz Tito, communist leader of Yugoslavia since 1945 died at age 88.

August - In Poland the Gdansk Agreement was signed after strikes that started at the Lenin Shipyards in that city. This allowed greater civil rights.

1981

January - Ronald Reagan became President of the United States and the Iran hostage crisis ended with the return of our citizens.

August - Libyan planes attacked US jets in the Gulf of Sidra, which Libya illegally annexed.

Barbara and I decided we didn't need such a large house now, especially with the two older boys (my painting assistants) out of the nest. We looked at property on water and found a contemporary house that had been made from a smaller 1920's house that had frontage on the Racquet River. An art professor had added a large living room and a kitchen with cathedral ceiling above it and the loft master bedroom. Plenty of space to entertain and the river waterfront made it great. We moved in that month.

October - A Soviet submarine ran aground near the Swedish naval base at Karlskrona.

December - Communist General Jaruzelski began martial law in Poland, restricting normal life. He was trying to crush the Solidarity trade union and opposition to communist rule.

1982

January - David started graduate school at SUNY Plattsburgh, working on a Master's in counseling.

February - President Reagan announced an initiative to prevent the overthrow of governments in the Caribbean Basin by communist forces.

April - Argentina invaded the Falkland Islands, opening the Falklands War with Britain.

May - Spain joined NATO.

Laurie Conroe graduated and received her nursing pin at SUNY Plattsburgh. She came home to Potsdam and began her career at the hospital there.

At SUNY Potsdam, both the President and the Academic Vice President were leaving. SUNY central office in Albany sent us a temporary President for a year, and I was on my own again running the Vice President's office. It all actually worked well.

June - Israel invaded Lebanon to stop raids from Syrian troops based there.

The Falkland Islands were liberated by a British task force, ending the War.

John Conroe graduated High School and prepared to enroll at SUNY Cortland with a major in Biology. Our educational plans for the younger generation seemed to be working and the economics thereof seem to be holding up as well.

October - Laurie is sure she has met the man of her dreams. We will see how that goes. Now John faces Draft registration, too.

November - Leonid Brezhnev died in the USSR and Yuri Andropov became General Secretary.

1983

January - Soviet spy Gerhardt was arrested in New York City.

March - President Reagan proposed the Strategic Defense Initiative ("Star Wars")

April - Laurie and Jim (the "fox" referred to in October) became engaged after said "fox" had asked for my blessing. They should be great together.

May - David finished his Master/s and went back to Southampton, where he worked at the Meadow Club at a low level job. After several events happened, he became Assistant Manager and ultimately Manager.

September - A civilian Korean airliner, carrying 269 passengers including a US Congressman, was shot down by a Soviet interceptor plane.

Laurie married Jim Mousaw in a wonderful ceremony followed by a very nice reception.

By now, Scott was working for the Auburn, NY, daily newspaper as a reporter, covering civic meetings and police activities.

A new President arrived at the College.

October - US forces invaded the Caribbean island of Grenada in order to overthrow the Marxist government, expel Cuban troops, and stop the construction of a Soviet-funded airstrip.

November - Soviet anti-aircraft personnel misinterpreted a NATO test of nuclear warfare procedures as be a fake cover for an actual attack. Soviet nuclear forces were then placed on high alert.

On December 16, Barbara's mother, Irene Holme, passed away, another major loss for our family. She was 82.

1984

January - The College President appointed one of the academic deans to be Acting Vice President for Academic Affairs, which was a relief.

February - Konstantin Chernenko was made General Secretary of the Soviet Communist Party replacing Andropov.

Scott had changed newspapers and was now writing for the Syracuse daily paper.

The College President and the Acting Vice President laid out a plan before me for something new at Potsdam, with me as the facilitator. They had both attended Harvard and appreciated the student residence plan of housing and were interested in establishing a theme house. The idea was to establish activities both social and/or supplementing the academic life. They asked me to design a program, design an apartment for a house "master" like at Harvard, implement the whole program and would Barbara and I be the house "parents."

I agreed and, after discussion with Barbara, accepted with the proviso that we not live with SUNY furniture. My mother-in-law had died the previous December, and we had her better-looking furniture plus extra furniture of our own.

May - David finished his Master's degree at SUNY Plattsburgh and returned to Southampton.

July - Allies of the Soviet Union boycotted the Olympic Summer Games to be held in Los Angeles.

August - A new Vice President arrived at the College. That title was changed to Provost, so mine became Vice Provost. I had become quite good at helping incoming Presidents and Vice Presidents become acclimated to the College by then. Student Affairs was moved under her responsibilities, so I had new responsibilities helping her oversee that fairly large operation.

September - Barbara and I moved into our 2-bedroom, 2-bath apartment, welcomed our voluntary students and acquired our campus meal tickets, so that we could have dinner with our students. It was quite successful, and I published a journal article about the process of establishing the house. I had designed the apartment using five student rooms. We would stay there for at least two years, and Laurie and Jim moved into our real house.

December - Prime Minister Margaret Thatcher and the UK government met with Mikhail Gorbachev of the USSR in England to open a dialog with Soviet leadership candidates.

1985

March - Gorbachev assumed the leadership of the Soviet Union.

July - On the 31st, Laurie and Jim welcomed the birth of their first child, Jenna Leigh. Now Barbara and I became grandparents. What a concept! We were thrilled.

August - On the 40th anniversary of the bombing of Hiroshima and Nagasaki, the USSR began what it called a 5-month moratorium on the testing of nuclear weapons. The US administration thought this was a propaganda move and didn't adopt the idea. Gorbachev extended it a few times, but the US still didn't go along, so the moratorium ended in February of 1987.

November - Gorbachev and our President Reagan met for the first time in Geneva and agreed on having at least two more summits in the future.

1986

February - France launched a military operation to repulse the Libyan invasion of Chad.

The People Power Revolution occurred in the Philippines. The dictator since 1965, Ferdinand Marcos was overthrown, and the first female president, Corazon Aquino, was sworn into office.
April - The United States bombed Libya.

The Chernobyl disaster occurred in the Soviet Union. A nuclear power plant exploded, creating the worst nuclear power plant accident in history.
May - John graduated from SUNY Cortland, having changed his major from Biology to Economics/Management. He came back to Potsdam and worked at a bank in Norfolk, just north of there.
June - Laurie and Jim had bought a house and moved out of ours, and we moved back in. I had also decided to retire, having turned 55 in April and becoming a little frustrated with the job and with the larger SUNY. Anyway, our youngest had finished college, and the potential pension looked good. Also, another new Vice President would be arriving in September.
October - At a summit of world leaders in Reykjavik, Iceland, a breakthrough in nuclear arms control was realized.

President Reagan signed into law an act of Congress which gave $100 million of aid, both military and humanitarian, to the Contras in Nicaragua. These were groups of rebels active from 1979 to the early 1900's. Later, US support was banned by Congress, but the Reagan administration continued it covertly, which eventually led to the Iran-Contra scandal.

Having taken early retirement, Barbara and I moved to Saratoga Springs so I would have more opportunities for part time educational work. It also put us nearer my elderly parents (40 miles south) and my unmarried older sister (40 miles west) so I could help any of the above.

As we prepared to leave Potsdam, the College President asked me to represent Potsdam College in a three-week swing through southeastern Asia with a group of representatives of other US colleges. We would visit American schools and talk with students from various countries attending them with regard to potential college admissions. The decision was a no-brainer, but it meant that Barbara would stay in a motel outside Saratoga Springs while our house there was under construction. She agreed that this was an opportunity that could not be ignored.

Traveling to seven countries and talking with many school officials and high students was fascinating and a real learning experience. We also talked with each country's young people about our colleges and reflected on their desire for information about educational options. That was a very valuable trip in so many ways.

November - The Iran-Contra affair erupted when the Reagan administration announced that it had been selling arms to Iran for the release of hostages and then transferring the profits illegally to the Nicaraguan Contras.

1987

In January, President Gorbachev was trying to get his economic redevelopment plan (Perestroika) going, but met with resistance from some members of the Communist Party.

In February, we joined a community theater group and I began part time jobs. Barbara began a long run as a hospital volunteer in the Emergency Department. She loved it.

President Reagan visited Berlin, Germany, in June, where, referring to the Berlin Wall, he made his speech that contained his famous "Mr. Gorbachev, tear down this wall."

In November, the Joint Congressional Investigating Committee, after a year of study and hearings into the Iran-Contra affair, issued its report. It amounted to a healthy slap on the wrist, stating that the administration acted with disdain for the law.

December brought another meeting between Presidents Reagan and Gorbachev, this time in Washington. They both signed the Intermediate-Range Nuclear Forces Treaty, which some people claimed that that was the end of the Cold War.

1988

This was both a good year and a hard year for our extended family. We had our highs and our lows, but overall survived it OK.

In February, David married Dianne Kujawa, with both the ceremony and the reception at her parents' house in Southampton. A happy occasion, and we instantly gained another granddaughter, Aura, Dianne's 8-year old daughter.

On the 22nd, two of our US navy ships were rammed off the coast of the Crimean peninsula. They were the USS Yorktown and the USS Caron. Both had wandered into territorial waters of the Soviet Union.

March joyfully brought us a third granddaughter. Laurie and Jim's second daughter, Kaylie Elizabeth, was born on her father's birthday, March 4.

Later that month, Barbara and I, my brother and his wife and my sister met together with our parents at their house. I had decided that it was time for them to sell their house and move to an apartment. They actually agreed, since Mother had had a hip replacement in January, and my niece and her husband who had been living with them would be moving out in May.

On May 15, Soviet troops began leaving Afghanistan.

Later in May, Dad had surgery at Albany Medical Center to install two aluminum bone supports in his left forearm and left thigh. His breast cancer had spread to the bones several months earlier. Luckily, I was able to make myself available for manning help and transportation.

In June, Barbara and I were able to take a two week tour to the Canadian Rockies plus Alaska to celebrate our 35th anniversary.

In July, my parents' house sold, and I began looking at apartments. Mother wondered if they could have separate apartments. Sadly, she was serious. I told her that they couldn't afford to do that. My niece found the right place - large enough for them and 15 miles nearer us.

Tragically, that month, my sister had a blood clot in her brain that required middle-of-the-night surgery in Schenectady, which required next of kin to sign for it. My niece took Mother there for that. After the surgery was deemed successful, she needed extended therapy, both physical and mental. It was difficult to find a hospital that would take her due to additional physical issues. A head injury hospital in Troy agreed to take her, if I signed for her as next of kin. It was all too much for my parents, so I became the hospital's contact.

August was the time to run a huge yard sale at my parents' house followed by their move northward. All went well.

During this time and into the fall, I was driving Dad to his oncology appointments and discussing the situation with the doctor who said it was time to think about Hospice care.

In October, Dad was formally referred to Hospice. We met with the personnel and learned how that would work. The nearest hospital with a Hospice unit was St. Peter's in Albany. We were trying to figure out how we would find helpers to come to them and help when Dad began bleeding internally. He was rushed to St. Peter's the next day and died that night. He was 89. The next day I went to my sister's hospital room on her birthday to tell her, which was very sad.

By November, my sister had shown sufficient progress to leave the hospital for Thanksgiving, which was a nice change. However, Mother had fallen at her apartment, so my brother came to look after her.

The brain injury hospital sent a team to Connie's house outside Gloversville to install railings and check what else needed doing before she could go home.

In early December, Connie went home with everything prepared ahead, including an oxygen machine.

December 22nd, South Africa withdrew from Namibia in south west Africa.

1989

In January, a second Gulf of Sidra incident occurred between the US and Libya. Also, George H. W. Bush, former US Vice President, became President of the United States.

On February 2, troops of the USSR withdrew from Afghanistan.

Later in the month, Barbara's maiden aunt, Agnes Holme died in Pennsylvania at the age of 96. We met Barbara's brother and his wife there to take care of her estate and belongings, as well as having a small service.

June 4 was the date of the massive massacre in Tiananment Square, Bejing, China.

Television coverage displayed the brutality for us. The whole world was shocked.

That same day, almost-free elections were held in Poland. There was a lack of support in the Communist party, and the Solidarity trade union won the available seats in the Parliament and 99% of the Senate.

In August, Tadeusz Mazowiecki was elected the leader of the first non-communist government in eastern European countries.

October 18th marked the day that the Hungarian constitution was amended to allow for a multi-party political system government and free elections. Also, it marked the end of the nearly 20-year reign of communist the leader, Erich Honecker in East Germany.

November showed more activities in the breakdown of communist dictatorships. There were revolutions in eastern Europe. The Berlin Wall was breached when a high ranking political figure, not knowing correct procedures, announced in East Berlin that the borders were open.

December 4, at the end of a summit meeting in Malta the US and USS presidents announced that a long-lasting era of peace was begun. Many people thought that was the officially the beginning of the end of the Cold War.

On the 14th, democracy was restored in Chile.

From the 16th to the 25th, revolution was fought in Romania. The communist regime of Nicolae Ceausescu was overthrown, and rioters executed him and his wife.

Romania had the distinction of being the only Eastern Bloc to so violently overthrow the communist government.

On December 29, Vaclav Havel was installed as President of the newly free Czechoslovakia. This was particularly interesting in light of our life in West Germany near the border. That was a great event!

CHAPTER NINETEEN

The War's End Is In Sight

1990

January - The first McDonald's restaurant opened in Russia, in Moscow.

March - Lithuania became an independent state.

May - Boris Yeltsin became President of Russia.

August - Iraq invaded Kuwait. That was the beginning of the Gulf War.

September - On the 15th, John married Robin Brown of Norfolk, NY, with many friends and family gathered for the ceremony and reception in Potsdam. Really great!

October - Germany was reunified, which was also important to those of us who served at the Iron Curtain.

1991 -

February - The Gulf War ended.

My widowed aunt, Alice Boyd, died at her home near Hudson, NY. I was her Executor, so was in charge of all arrangements - funeral with reception (burial would be later), executing her will, giving others the gifts she had listed, emptying her house, and looking after her rental properties.

July - the Warsaw Pact of the Eastern Bloc was dissolved formally.

August - An attempted coup in the Soviet Union in response to a new union treaty due to be signed.

December - Our first and only grandson was born on the 21st. Laurie gave birth to Ryan Aaron Mousaw. If you have been keeping score, dear reader, we then had three granddaughters and one grandson. My, were we proud.

On the 25th, two major world events occurred. After speaking by phone with Russia's Boris Yeltsin, US President George H.W. Bush gave a Christmas Day speech stating that the Cold War had officially ended.

The other event that day was the resignation of Mikhail Gorbachev as President of the USSR. The hammer and sickle flag would be seen no more.

The next day, the Council of Republics of the Supreme Soviet of the USSR dissolved itself after recognizing the end of the Soviet Union.

On the 31st, all operations of Soviet institutions ceased.

Forty six years of world wide upheaval came to an end, but that was not the end of wars around the globe, by any means.

Thank you, dear reader, for staying with me through this long narration.

AFTERWARD

The world heaved a sigh of relief in 1991, when the Cold War was officially over.

Had we really learned from it? Evidently not. Since then there have been the Iraqi War, the Afghanistan War, the catastrophic attack on the World Trade Center, and, now, Vladimir Putin, the controller of Russia, is annexing the Crimea. He probably has his eye on other former USSR territory as well. In a recent opinion piece, correspondent George Will recently headed the column "Is the Ukraine the Cold War's final episode?".

Evidently, men and women, like children, will never be able to stamp out greed, avarice, envy and the want for someone else's "toys". But life goes on even as we witness terror attacks, gunfire in schools, and nature's way of reminding us that we are small beings when up against fires, floods and earthquakes.

The Conroe family has grown. John and Robin are parents of two girls, Emilee and Allison, David and Dianne are grandparents of two girls and two boys up in Maine, Scott is writing his first novel, and Laurie is now a certified nurse-midwife still in Potsdam. She and Jim are proud of their three for finishing college, finding jobs and now planning some weddings.

We are slowly reconciling ourselves to the reality of Barbara's loss. We are also praying that a cure for Alzheimer's Disease will be found so that other families will not have to experience the pain of that malady.

Bruce Conroe, March, 2014

APPENDIX

Losses Suffered By Hungary Through Escaped Refugees

In his book, "The Bridge at Andau", James Michener wrote of the tragedy for Hungary when numbers of very capable people escaped into the welcoming arms of westerners during the Hungarian uprising of 1956. At that time he was a correspondent for the international press. He wrote," Consider, for example, eleven groups that had left their homeland, and imagine the loss they represented to a nation."[*]

One, at the university in Sopron five hundred students, thirty-two professors and their entire families simply gave up all hope of a decent life under communism and came across the border. Canada's University of British Columbia accepted the entire group.

Two, the finest ballerina of the Budapest Opera walked out with several of her assistants.

Three, enough football players fled Hungary to make several teams of world-champion caliber.

Four, the three finest Gypsy orchestras of Hungary came out in a body and began to play around the restaurants of Europe.

---

[*] "The Bridge at Andau", James Michener, reprinted 1986 by Fawcett, pp.202 and 203.

Five, some of the top mechanics in the factories at Csepel left and were eagerly grabbed up by firms in Germany, Switzerland and Sweden.

Six, a staggering number of trained engineers and scientists in almost all phases of industry and research fled. Michener said that he met accidentally at least fifty engineers under the age of thirty and thought a careful census would reveal a few thousand more.

Seven, a majority of both the Budapest symphony orchestras came out and several of the best conductors came with them.

Eight, Many of Hungary's best artists fled across the border.

Nine, as did many of her notable writers.

Ten, several members of the Hungarian Olympic team decided to stay in Australia. Others defected along the way home.

Eleven, most impressive of all were the young couples with babies. No group crossed the bridge into Austria without its quota of young families. They were aided by brave doctors who gave them medicines so their babies would sleep quietly during the escape.